The gift-wrappe

'If you can't stop he

with the cows' gras

Sell Arum, the Mitchell family's unpredictable pony! But horrifying though the idea was, Dad meant it. So all the family plunged into a 'Save Arum' campaign – with some unexpected results and a final glorious climax.

A splendid story about a farming family in whose life horses matter – but so do cows.

Anne Farrell

The gift-wrapped pony

KNIGHT BOOKS
Hodder & Stoughton

For my sister, Sally, who reckoned I could do it

ISBN 0 340 21622 0

First published in Great Britain in 1974 by Brockhampton Press Ltd (now Hodder & Stoughton Children's Books), in association with Hodder & Stoughton (Australia) Pty Ltd.

This edition first published in 1977.

Printed and bound in Great Britain in Knight Books for Hodder & Stoughton Children's Books, a division of Hodder & Stoughton Ltd, Arlen House, Salisbury Road, Leicester, by Cox & Wyman Ltd, London, Reading and Fakenham.

Contents

I *Wayward Grey Pony*

Saturday: at first the morning was perfect, with light wind, dazzling sunshine and a wide, unblemished sky. Though maybe a cloudless sky was a bit lacking in character, Lesley thought as she dawdled along the dairy track, waiting for Val to come and help feed the calves. But the good weather was well timed, for her father was ready to cut the hay. The Mitchells' ancient farm machinery was unreliable enough without the complication of uncertain weather. Harvest time at Guara was always exciting, though every year Lesley was a little sorry to see the splendid hay paddocks divested of their proud, knee-high crop and left with nothing but stalky dry stubble.

Thinking of this rather wistfully, she turned to look at the rolling green waves of the Home Paddock, and suddenly froze with horror. Arum, the family's wayward grey pony, was actually grazing in the middle of them.

'Oh, no! Val! *Val*!' she called urgently, and began running down the track.

Val appeared at the back gate, barefoot, still buttoning her shirt. She grasped the situation with one horrified glance, but had the presence of mind to dash back for a halter before tearing after her younger sister to the gate of the Home Paddock, which had been left open in readiness for the tractor and mower. From this point they could see everything: the nipped-off grass near the gateway of the paddock, the trail of trampled, flattened grass that marked the escapee's progress and Arum herself, who had lifted her head at their approach and somehow still managed to look innocent even though stalks of forbidden food stuck out each side of her whiskery grey muzzle, and grass that was sacred for hay gently tickled her black tummy.

'How could she!' groaned Val. 'Dad will be absolutely livid! I thought she'd be perfectly safe in the orchard.'

'Well, never mind that now. Just help me get her out of here before Dad sees her.'

They picked their way gingerly towards Arum, keeping to her track and trying not to increase the damage that she had already done. The pony blinked at them amiably, making no objection when Lesley slipped the halter over her head, and submitting docilely to being led away from the scene of her crime.

'How like her,' Val complained, 'to get into the best hay paddock just before it's due to be cut. David says she's half-witted, but I think she must be just the opposite to manage this.'

'She's neither, really. I mean, she's awfully clever the way she gets through fences, but jolly dopey not to have learnt by now that she always gets shut up when she does it.'

At the gate they turned back, gloomily surveying the devastation, and Lesley felt a wild, foolish desire to rush back into the paddock and prop up every trampled blade of grass. But Val, who was the quicker thinker and usually more practical, had realized the futility of any repair measures quite two minutes ago, and was busy on the problem of What to Do with Arum.

'We obviously can't put her back in the orchard. Even if we shut all the hay paddock gates (which Dad wouldn't like), there's still a lot of other damage she could do if she got out again.'

'And it can't be the Pony Paddock yet,' added Lesley, 'because the fence is still all trampled where she walked through it last time.'

'Then it will have to be the stable, for now, and a working bee on the fence after breakfast,' Val decided. 'Come on, Old 'Arum Scarum!'

Arum lowered her plain, bony head and came on obligingly, her unshod hooves constantly endangering Val's bare heels. Her shoulder was bony, too, most uncomfortable for barebacked riding, but elsewhere she was well-rounded, with a Joseph coat that ranged from white to black. The white was on her nose like a snowfall, and the black began behind her grey shoulder and continued to her rump, where her tail was black too, at the base, but white at the tip, with descending shades of grey in between. The Mitchells put it in a nutshell and called her a grey, but in winter she flouted even this all-embracing term by growing a thick coat of rusty brown. Her ears, however, were always grey, as well as being outsized and furry and the wrong shape, just like arum lilies; hence her name.

A calf bellowed from its shed, reminding Val and Lesley of what they should be doing.

'Hurry up,' said Val. 'Whack her on the rump, Les.'

Lesley did, and one of the clumsy hooves found its mark on Val's bare foot.

'Aa-oow! My foot!' She thrust the halter rope at Lesley and bent down to apply her handkerchief to the grazed toe. 'Look at the gore! I'll get tetanus or something, and it'll be all your fault, you unspeakable horse!'

Val shook her fist at Arum, who blinked, then replaced the bloodstained handkerchief in her shorts pocket. 'Sacred to the memory of my dear, departed toe, mourned by his nine brothers and sadly missed!'

Lesley began to giggle, but stopped as Val hobbled ahead to open the stable door.

'Hold on. Hadn't we better go and see how she got out of the orchard? I mean, the fences there are pretty good. She must have made a terrible mess of them to get into the Home Paddock.'

'Oh, heck, yes, I'd forgotten that. Don't put her away yet, we'll take her along. Perhaps if we give her a good whipping on the spot she got out she might get the connection.

'You wouldn't!'

Val grinned and slapped Arum on the rump. 'Of course not. But *you* lead her. *I'm* going to walk at least ten paces behind!'

By half past eight, all but one of the Mitchell family were assembled for breakfast in the big room that was referred to as the kitchen, although really a good half of it was dining-room, occupied by a heavy wooden table and six creaky chairs. At the kitchen end of the room Mrs Mitchell, medium-sized and dark, was cooking bacon to the great delight of her two cats, Possum and Catkin, who were sitting pointedly on either side of her. Val, at fourteen, looked ridiculously like her mother except that her dark-brown hair was longer and perpetually tied in two untidy bunches under her ears. Lesley, on the other hand, was fairish like her father, while David, their sixteen-year-old brother, was fair with no ish about it; his hair was rather like disorderly straw, growing just a little longer than his father liked.

Mr Mitchell was sitting at the head of the table listening sceptically to Val's explanation of the destruction in the Home Paddock, which he had noticed on his way in from milking.

'She opened the gate?' he said incredulously, after several comments so grim that his placid wife had begun to look worried. But Val was so delighted with the rare intelligence Arum had showed that she refused to feel subdued.

'We went back to have a look at the orchard fences to see where she'd got out this time,' she was saying excitedly. 'And they were all right! But the gate was open —'

'So I said she must have let herself out,' continued Lesley. 'But Val said —'

'To cut a long story short,' Val interrupted hastily, 'we put her in again and shut the gate, and she *opened* it!'

'But how?' asked David blankly, getting on with his cornflakes as he listened.

'You know how the orchard gate is just a section of the fence with a wire loop to hold the end dropper to the corner post?' said Val – mainly for her mother's benefit, as her father and David had fenced it themselves – 'Well, she just stuck her nose in the gap between the dropper and post and shoved upwards till the wire was off the dropper and the whole gate collapsed.'

'Then she picked her way over it like someone in white shoes crossing a mucky yard,' added Lesley, grinning. 'Still think she's half-witted, David?'

'Of course,' said David with conviction. 'She ended up shut in the stable, didn't she? And I know how we can stop her opening gates,' he added, accepting a plate of bacon and eggs from his mother. 'If you drive a nail halfway into the side of the dropper and fasten the wire loop *below* it, that will stop the loop coming off when she shoves.' He was the most practical member of the family, and would be leaving school at the fast-approaching end of the year, to give his father much-needed assistance on the farm.

Much-needed assistance was what Mr Mitchell was talking about now.

'The hay's ready to be cut,' he was saying to David, 'so I'll need some help overhauling the machinery today. And I'll have to see about some extra labour for carting in. We can't really afford it, but we'll have to, especially as you'll probably be still at school.

'I've never known such a dry November,' he added, and turned to Val and Lesley. 'Be a good idea for you to tie that cranky mare where she can clean up some of the long grass along the lanes before it gets to be a fire hazard. It'll be all she'll get for a while; I haven't time to fix up the fence in her paddock yet.' He paused, then said seriously, 'If you can't stop her getting loose and playing havoc with the cows' grass and hay, she'll have to be sold. I know she was bought for you kids, but we can't keep her if she goes on costing money all over the place.'

Lesley and Val, and even David, looked horrified at this, but the subject was dropped as ten-year-old Ian, the last of the Mitchells, burst into the kitchen flourishing the newspaper he had gone out to collect from the mail-box at the boundary fence. He handed it to his father first, as ritual demanded, then collapsed in front of his cornflakes and announced the headline news to the rest of the family.

'There's been a big fire! Out at Valleywood last night. Two big barns burned down and a lot of other things, and the police think it was lit on purpose!'

For once Ian had everyone's attention. Valleywood was the name of McGuire's Jersey stud, famous in Tasmania, and well-known even in other states of Australia.

It was only ten miles away from Guara. The dream of every breeder of registered Jerseys (including Jim Mitchell) was one day to own a herd like Jock McGuire's.

'Cripes!' said David, getting up to look at the newspaper over his father's shoulder.

'Who on earth would want to do that?' cried Val, craning her neck to see too.

'They're pretty vague on that,' said Ian informatively, anxious to keep his audience, 'but it does say it was last year's hay in the barns, so it couldn't have been spontaneous combustion after such a long time.'

Lesley pushed back her chair to have a look too, but her father noticed and said, 'Nobody else breathing down my neck, *please*. I'll pass it on when I've finished.' So she started clearing the table as if that had been her intention anyway.

'Hey, don't take the milk yet,' complained Ian. 'And I'll want some salt for my bacon and eggs if you greedy lot saved me any. I suppose you knew,' he added maddeningly, 'that Arum's in the chook-yard, trimming down the willow-tree?'

Lesley, with one horrified glance at her father, dropped the salt and fled. Val gulped down her scalding cup of tea and jumped up too. Her mother said understandingly, 'It's all right, dear, I'll do the washing-up, but you'd better wire up the stable latch this time.'

David looked at the clock, then at his father immersed in the paper. 'I've got a minute. I'll come and help you prop up the Pony Paddock fence, if you like.'

'Oh, thanks,' said Val. 'Coming, Ian?'

'What, after running all the way from the mail-box in this heat? And I haven't even finished my breakfast yet.'

Lesley heard this from the veranda and wondered how

Ian could be so unconcerned. Then she remembered that he had come in late for breakfast and hadn't heard their father say that if Arum didn't stop escaping, she would soon be gone for good.

2 Fence menders

The Pony Paddock, separated from the Mitchells' garden by only the fowl-yard, was much more attractive than the square, monotonous cow pastures and calf paddocks that made up the rest of the farm. But the charm of the ancient, leaning wooden stable and the staid but shady old weeping willow that drooped behind it was lost even on Lesley this morning. And it was doubtful whether any of the other Mitchells ever noticed anything but the decrepit fence that separated Arum from her dangerous freedom.

The fence had originally been designed for calves. It had posts at each corner, but only thin wooden droppers in between to hold up the sagging sheep-wire and the slack top line of barbed-wire. Even so, a normal horse, with a normal horse's distrust of wire, would have had a healthy respect for it. Arum hadn't. When she had grazed down the drying grass of her paddock and trimmed the weeping willow as far as she could reach, she took to leaning heavily against the fence and stretching her long neck to reach grass in the two adjoining paddocks. After a fair bit of leaning, the fence had given way enough to be walked over, although sometimes she got her soup-plate hooves tangled in the sheep-wire and had to stand there patiently until someone noticed, and helped her out by holding the wires apart with one hand and with the other extricating each black leg in turn.

After several of these incidents the fence was in a pretty sorry state. Val and Lesley surveyed it in despair when they arrived armed with a couple of hammers, a lot of staples, and some extra wire. But David had helped his father with fencing before; he took command authoritatively. He had managed to find a few old steel droppers, and gave directions for them to be bashed into the ground to reinforce the weakest part of the fence.

'But the ground's so dry,' Val objected. 'You could hardly bash a needle into it!'

David said did she want the fence fixed or didn't she, and to just shut up and help Lesley brace the dropper while he bashed it in. But this was hopeless. It was like trying to drive the dropper through solid rock. David was nonplussed for a moment. Lesley kicked the shoes off her hot feet, rested her jolted arms and gazed at the fence for inspiration.

'It sort of wants a few tucks taking in it,' she said thoughtfully, 'or a tourniquet at each end. It'd be plenty high enough if we could only get it to stand up straight.'

'It wants re-straining, only there isn't a straining post,' said David. 'And it wants re-wiring, only there isn't any more wire. In fact, it wants totally re-fencing!'

'If only it could be,' Val sighed. 'With white posts and a single white rail on top, like a proper horse fence.'

'A single rail? You must be joking! Arum would gnaw through that before you drove the last nail in. That mare's a cross between Houdini and a beaver!'

'That makes her a Hou-ver,' said Lesley, trying it out.

'Jolly appropriate! She cleans up everything like a plague of locusts when she gets out.'

Lesley turned to check that Arum was still tied securely to the fence where they had left her, and beheld her younger brother running across from the house.

'Look at Ian. I wonder what's up.'

'Not coming to help anyway,' said Val cynically. 'Not at that lick!'

Ian cast himself down in the shade of the willow, fanning his face with the morning newspaper.

'Gosh, you haven't done much! Dad wants you, David. You're to go back straight away.'

'Ready to start on the mower, I s'pose,' said David, going.

'*Now*,' said Val, descending on Ian with a hammer. 'Get up and help us with this fence!'

Ian stopped fanning and held up his fan enticingly. 'Here's the paper,' he said. 'Don't you want to read all about the fire?'

He lay back peacefully while they read the account of the fire and studied the two dramatic photos. Then he saw Val's eye stray back to the fence and produced his trump card. 'Dad's bought six heifers from the Valleywood place and he's getting them this morning.'

'*What?*'

Ian said it again, more slowly, and added, 'That's what he wanted David for, to help get the sides on the land-rover.'

To illustrate this point, the Mitchells' long-wheel-base land-rover bounced down the farm road in a cloud of dust, its portable sides rattling alarmingly. Val stared, then flopped down under the willow beside Ian. 'I give up,' she said. 'Tell us all, you little horror.'

'It was just after you lot all rushed out here,' he explained. 'Dad had a phone call from Mr McGuire. Apparently Dad ordered some heifers from him ages ago, when he started the stud, but there was a waiting list a yard long and he didn't expect to get any for years and years. But apparently Mr McGuire's place is all messed up after that fire and he's selling all his heifers to cope.

And he offered Dad six if he'd take them right away.'

'And *apparently* he said he would,' murmured Val in amazement, gazing at the departing dust cloud.

But Lesley burst out indignantly, 'Six new heifers! Just like that, after all the talk about not being able to afford things and selling Arum!'

'Selling Arum?' Ian was finally shocked into sitting up.

Val explained. 'And that's why we all dashed out here to mend her fence quick-smart, and that's why *you* are now going to apply your wits and energy to helping us complete the job!'

'It really wants re-fencing completely,' said Ian helpfully.

'That's what David said,' replied Lesley witheringly. 'A fat lot of use our brothers are!'

'Shut up a minute, Les,' Val said thoughtfully. 'What was it you were saying, before Ian came out?'

Lesley thought back and remembered. 'That it needed a tuck in it?'

'No, the other thing . . . A tourniquet, that's it! I think it just might work.'

And, oddly enough, it did. A short, strong stick twisted around the top wire, tourniquet-style, tightened it up very smartly, and gave the fence a much more business-like appearance.

'Now for the sheep-wire,' said Val exultantly.

Ian cheerfully helped her find some more sticks, but Lesley worked in silence, several worries crowding for top priority in her mind. The fence was looking quite hopeful now, but dear, scatty Arum might even jump it if she couldn't lean it into submission. Lesley glanced at the beloved, ungainly pony in the lane and suddenly allowed a long-suppressed thought to rise to the forefront of her mind.

Another pony.

Arum had been bought when they were all much younger for David and Val to learn to ride on, but now that David was growing out of her, she was really Val's responsibility. Lesley and Ian could both ride, of course, but neither was allowed to take Arum off the farm alone. Ian didn't care much, though he was fond of old 'Arum Scarum and quite liked riding, but it was a thorn in Lesley's side that whenever she wanted Arum, Val always seemed to need her more urgently – to ride into the town for something, to train her over an improvised set of jumps, to try a new method of schooling she had read about, or to go to see a friend. Lesley wasn't selfish; she didn't grudge Val her pony or envy her the extra responsibility of being older, but secretly, for quite a long time, she had longed for a pony of her own. A pony to look after, to train, to ride whenever she liked, to be all *her* responsibility. Her father had his cattle dog, Tassel, her mother the two spoiled cats, David had the whole herd of cows as his main interest, Ian had two guinea pigs, and Val had Arum, but somehow she had no special animal at all.

There was a more practical side to the picture, too. Another pony would be company for Arum and most likely prevent her from escaping through places where a more conventional creature would not follow.

But balancing these factors, in fact hopelessly over-balancing them, was the dark, looming problem of finance. First it had been farm machinery, then a new barn and dairy. Now it was building up a herd of registered Jerseys, as if ordinary old cows weren't good enough to produce milk. Lesley tugged viciously at the wire she was tightening. The six new heifers this morning would be the very end. She remembered once hearing her father say wistfully that Jock McGuire charged two hundred dollars for springing heifers, and suddenly she had a horrible thought. Supposing he sold Arum to help meet this unexpected expense? The idea was so terrible that she let go her tourniquet altogether, and the wire she was tightening sprang back into slackness.

'What's bitten you?' said Ian, looking up in surprise.

Lesley hesitated. She had never mentioned any of this before, but the sudden, shocking thought was too awful to be borne alone. She found herself voicing it to Val and Ian, then plunged in and rushed on to tell them about her plan.

'Another pony!' yelped Val in astonishment. 'When Dad's threatened to sell the one we've already got? You must be absolutely bonkers!'

'But you know what ponies are like,' protested Lesley. 'When they get matey they hate to lose sight of each other, and there can't be another pony in Australia that would go through these fences after Arum.'

'So she'd just have to stay in,' said Ian, seeing what she meant.

'But that's not the point!' said Val exasperatedly. 'You can't possibly expect Dad to pay money for another pony so that we can keep the one we've got – which, for all we know, he may be planning to sell to pay for these heifers anyway.'

'I suppose *you* know what you mean,' said Ian doubtfully, but Lesley went on tying her tourniquet with some bale twine and said nobody had even suggested Dad should buy another pony. Everyone was raising money for something these days, she said, so why couldn't they? It didn't have to be an expensive show pony or anything.

While Val digested this, Ian had an idea and rushed over to the willow-tree to get his newspaper. He spread it on the ground and leafed through to the *Wanted to Sell* page.

'Pony mare, 12 h.h., 7 years . . .'

Lesley and Val leant down to look too, but Val soon realised the absurdity of reading advertisements like 'Wanted to Sell, Show Jumper, 15 h.h., $250.'

'We have to find the money before the horse,' she said, and turned back to *Positions Vacant*.

' "Experienced waiter, experienced taxi-driver, reliable dressmaker, experienced secretary . . ." The trouble is,' she said presently, 'we're not experienced anythings.'

'Except fence-menders,' said Lesley, grinning. 'Thanks to my tourniquet method. I might patent that and make pots of money!'

'Here's someone who made pots of money,' said Ian, still leafing through the newspaper and now reading the official Tattersals lottery results. 'Twenty-five thousand dollars in one fell swoop. We could buy another farm and stock it with horses. Let's get a ticket in Tatts!'

'We want something much more certain than that,' said Val scathingly, taking the paper from him and holding back her hair to see better. 'Hey, Les, get a load of this.' She stabbed at the page with a finger and Lesley read aloud: ' "Under eighteens, have you posted your entries for the end-of-year prose and poetry collection to be compiled by noted local author" . . . Never heard of him,' she finished, looking up.

'I have,' said Val, 'and I must say he sounds a bit whacky to be doling out twenty-dollar prizes to kids for stuff they wrote in English exercises. But what I meant was, it's your thing, writing, and – well, twenty dollars – you ought to have a go. What do you have to do?'

Lesley scanned the column. 'He wants stories and poems and essays written by local kids during the year. It says they *can* be school exercises, as long as they're original. He wants to pick out good ones to publish in some book or other, and there are prizes for the best in each age-group. What a weird turn-out! Anyway, I'm sure none of my school compositions would do —'

'Well, write one that will do,' interrupted Val. 'I think you should try, at least.'

'I don't think it's any more hopeful than Tatts,' Lesley objected; but her glance strayed back to the age-groups bit. It was true, writing was her favourite thing, though she didn't have much time to do it out of school. 'Under thirteen,' she murmured. 'I s'pose I might try a story, but there isn't much time.'

'You write one, and let me read it when you've finished,' ordered Val. 'What a pity there isn't a drawing section for me. I'm hopeless at writing.'

'I'm hopeless at both,' said Ian cheerfully, starting to pick up hammers and left-over wire, 'but you never know, I might turn out to be a terrific Experienced Hairdresser Apply in Writing!'

Lesley squashed him with a glance and rolled up the newspaper while Val went to get Arum and turn her loose in her paddock. 'Best to do it in the morning, then if she does get out, we'll probably see her before she can Houver anything.' Her voice changed to a more urgent note. 'Hurry up, you two. Dad's back. I can see the landrover at the stockyards. Who's coming to get an eyeful of these toffee-nosed heifers?'

3 *Valleywood Gipsy*

Everyone came, and even Lesley was impressed by the sleek-coated, golden young Jerseys with a similar special, high-class look about them that thoroughbred horses have. She began to understand why her father was so keen to breed pedigree Jerseys from animals like these rather than the mixed bag of crossbreds that made up a large part of the Guara herd. But Val exclaimed, 'Gosh, they're not very big, are they?' and all Ian said was, had they found out who lit the fire yet?

'No,' David told Ian, and to Val, as the heifers picked their way down the leading ramp into the holding yard, he said, 'They're only yearlings. Quite a bit cheaper than incalf heifers, and Mr McGuire reduced the price even more because Dad agreed to take them before he was really ready for them.'

Lesley digested this information with relief, then climbed up to sit on the fence between Ian and her mother, while Mr Mitchell pointed out each heifer individually.

'I can't remember all the details Jock told me,' he was saying, 'but we'll be getting their pedigrees soon, anyway.

'The dark one in the corner is out of Valleywood Romany, top-producing Jersey in the State for five years. She's getting on a bit now, of course, but we saw her today, and she's still a fine old cow. That fire was a stroke of luck for us, really. Jock would never have sold a daughter of old Romany if it hadn't been for that. This heifer will make a terrific cow, and you wouldn't get better blood-lines to build a stud anywhere.'

'What's her name?' asked Lesley, reluctantly admiring the alert brown eyes in the heifer's broad, dished face, her near-perfect body lines, and the warm colour of her silky coat that gleamed like polished wattle-wood.

'Valleywood Gipsy,' replied her father, closing gates while David drove the heifers into the lane.

'They certainly are a beautiful line,' remarked Mrs Mitchell, watching them go. 'Much better than the first purebreds we bought, Jim.'

'No doubt about that, but I still don't think we can really afford them.'

His wife sighed with the air of one who has been through this before. She had, in fact, spent half an hour over the breakfast table talking him into buying the heifers. 'You know they'll pay for themselves in no time when they come in milk,' she assured him patiently.

'That's right, I suppose,' he agreed, not wanting to get dragged into the discussion all over again. 'Now, will you kids take them the rest of the way and shut them in the Bottom Calf Paddock, where we can keep an eye on them? There's only about an hour before dinner, and David and I already have two hours' work to squeeze into it.'

Ian said he was going fishing with some other boys in the afternoon and had to fix up his guinea-pig cage before then, or they'd get out, but Val and Lesley agreed to take the heifers, and Mrs Mitchell joined them as they trailed Gipsy, Sonnet, Mimosa, Ruby, Trinket and Dainty down the dusty track. Tassel, the kelpie-cross cattle dog, came too, hopefully on the lookout for breakaways, but the six heifers were perfectly decorous and somewhat aloof, like six beauty queens fully conscious of the honour they were conferring on Guara.

In complete contrast to this, their behaviour when they reached the paddock was quite astonishing. First a few cautious steps, then several sniffs, and suddenly they were galloping round the new territory, bucking with excitement, their tasselled tails streaming behind them. All around the perimeter ('Like a lap of honour,' said Val), then a screeching halt at the other end to goggle at the milking herd, who goggled back at them over the fence of the cow pasture. Another wheeling take-off and they were pounding up the paddock again, stopping this time to touch noses through the fence with the winter calves in the next-door calf paddock. The calves caught the excitement, and when the heifers turned to tear back down the paddock, they galloped along in sympathy, though the fence was between them. When the newcomers finally flagged, out of breath, and began sampling the spring grass, Val and Lesley and their mother were quite helpless from laughing at them.

'It's the funniest thing I've seen for ages,' gasped Mrs Mitchell, turning back to the house. 'My word, you did a good job with the fence,' she added, as they passed the Pony Paddock.

Arum lumbered up to meet them while Lesley was showing her mother the tourniquets, and presented her snowflake nose to be rubbed. Just time for a ride before dinner, Val thought to herself, rubbing it. But before she could turn back to the stable for Arum's bridle, Mrs Mitchell exclaimed, 'Heavens, just look at the time! I should be getting the dinner on. Val, will you pull me some carrots and parsnips from the garden, please? And some beans. And I think we'll have fruit salad, since it's so hot.'

Val sighed and headed for the vegetable garden, but

Lesley went inside with her mother. She had an idea for a story, and if she could only find a pen that would write, there would be time to start it before dinner.

She found a pen, but after half an hour's scribbling and scratching-out and brain-racking, she realised that a pen that would work, even when coupled with an urgent reason for writing, was not much good without inspiration. She was glad when it was dinner time. The fresh young vegetables with cold meat made a welcome interval, and the fruit salad and cream were pleasantly cool in such humid weather. When dinner was over, Mr Mitchell and David hurried out to get the mower going and Ian collected his fishing-rod and rushed off to meet his friends. Val and Lesley washed up, as they had been excused this chore at breakfast time, and their mother put on shorts and a sun-hat and went outside to do mysterious things in her beloved vegetable garden.

'I don't know how she can potter round in all this heat,' said Val, forgetting that she had wanted to go riding. 'I wouldn't like to be Dad on the tractor, either. Come swimming down at the Willow Hole when we've finished here?'

'No,' said Lesley. 'I'm too busy.'

'Oh, come on! David's helping Dad, and Ian's already gone off somewhere.' The young Mitchells were not allowed to swim in the river alone.

'No, I've got to get on with my story,' said Lesley decisively, drying the last of the spoons and firmly squashing the luxurious thought of wallowing in the shade-cooled water under the willows. 'You're the one who told me to write it, and it's your pony we're trying to save.'

'It's your pony we're trying to buy, though,' Val

grumbled, wiping down the sink. Still in a bad mood, but reproaching herself for being inconsistent and ungrateful, she gloomily looked for something to read, then went outside to loll under the willow.

Lesley's story got on a bit better in the afternoon. Everyone else was outside, so there were no distractions except the sound of the tractor as Mr Mitchell mowed the grass in the Home Paddock, and this was far enough away to be no more than a persistent hum, more soothing than distracting.

Lesley knew the adage about sticking to familiar things, and had set her story on Shale Hill, which was historical and interesting and right on Guara's southern boundary. But she was beginning to realize that it wasn't really all that familiar; the hill was out-of-bounds to the young Mitchells. A lot of things other kids do are out-of-bounds for us, she thought, tapping her pen on her pad. So she went ahead and gave her imagination free rein, and the children in her story had a supremely exciting time exploring the disused shale mines, dropping things down the eight-foot ventilation shafts, getting lost in the bush, and falling in the river. Then she thought perhaps it ought to be toned down a bit to be more like real life, dreary and worrying though that was, and so she began a new, more subdued draft, introducing more descriptive passages and ruthlessly chopping out some of the adventures. Finally, with most of the afternoon over, she read the completed story through with satisfaction, stretched her legs, which had fallen asleep, and went out to find Val.

After only a few minutes in the deep shade of the weeping-willow, Val felt quite cool, and decided it might be tolerable to move out to the lawn and sunbake. Not too close to the vegetable garden, though, or she might be coerced into weeding the onions or something. The *Women's Weekly* was not madly interesting, but she had finished her library book, so she turned, as was her custom, to look up readable things in the contents column; readable things being, (a) anything to do with horses, (b) anything to do with cooking and food, and (c) anything to do with drawing or painting. Items in the first category were sadly lacking, so she read the recipes for party pavlovas (which set up hunger pains, though she had just had dinner), then brightened at a page of colourful oil paintings displayed by a plump little grey-haired lady who was obviously responsible for them.

But they weren't oil paintings but *Bark Paintings*, the headline announced, made by Mrs So-and-so from New South Wales. Val shielded her eyes from the sun's glare and had another look at the pictures. Her first thought was that she had been misled; they couldn't possibly be bark; but closer scrutiny showed her that the contrasting textures of those most attractive landscapes were indeed strips of bark, so beautifully arranged that they could have fooled anybody into thinking they were oils. There must be some way of colouring bark, Val thought, turning back to the script, but she was astonished again. Grey-haired Mrs So-and-so claimed that barks were the poor man's oils; the textures and colours were perfectly natural; glue was all you needed to make use of them. She went on to explain that ti-tree bark was best, but that any kind of tree with bark that peeled off readily would yield suitable material for a bark painter.

Val read on, thoroughly absorbed; what really impressed her most were the captions under the paintings – one had sold for twenty dollars, another for thirty dollars, a third for as much as fifty dollars. 'That settles it,' she thought. 'Tons of ti-trees in the River Paddock and I never noticed their bark, never even heard of bark paintings. Doesn't cost a cent, so there's nothing to lose if I can't do it. And all afternoon to find out if I can.'

She jumped up, and remembered to put the *Women's Weekly* away before dashing out to get Arum. The river Paddock was just too far away to walk, on a day like this.

'She did go off riding, but I'm sure I heard her come back hours ago,' Mrs Mitchell said in reply to Lesley's exasperated question. 'I don't know where she is now.' She straightened up, wiped her forehead, then took off the blue sun-hat which had been knocked askew by the gesture and fanned her face with it. 'I think I'll go in and get a drink from the fridge. You look nice and cool, darling. What have you been doing?'

Lesley was saved from replying by David, who rushed down the garden to meet them, saying, 'Thank goodness I've found someone. Dad's going to keep on mowing till the daylight gives out – he says it'd be asking for it to stop when the tractor's going so well, so I came back to milk.' He paused to down a large glass of iced cordial handed out by his mother. 'Anyway, one of the cows hasn't come home and I can't send Tassel down to run her up because she's due to calve soon.'

'Which cow?' asked Mrs Mitchell, pouring him another drink.

'Sharon, one of the purebreds. It'll be the first of the summer calves. Dad says we can rear it if it's a bull, as she's such a good breeding cow. I'm late already, so I dashed down to find someone to get her. Where the heck are Val and Ian?'

'Ian's gone fishing with the Frasers, and I don't know

where Val is. I'll go and get Sharon if you like,' offered Lesley, 'and if I see either of the others I'll send them back to help you milk.'

'O.K. Make sure you don't hurry her,' said David, referring to Sharon. 'But if she's already calved, leave her there. It'd probably be too heavy for you to carry. She's in Number Seven, right at the bottom, I'm afraid.' He put down his glass, grabbed an apple from the kitchen, and was gone. Lesley would have dashed after him, but her mother called her back.

'Put some shoes on first dear. You can't go all that way with nothing on your feet.'

Lesley's mind cast back desperately, trying to remember when the heat of the day had caused her to discard her shoes. In the Pony Paddock, when they were fencing; she remembered: she must have left them there. Blast! She turned and dashed in the other direction, and ran slap-bang into Val, who was sauntering out of the stable.

'Mind out, Les!' Val was shielding something in her hand.

'I've got to go and get a cow from Number Seven. And David's looking for you to help him milk. Where on earth have you been? And what's that you've got?'

'I'll show you later, since you're in such a rush. By the way, I found your shoes when I put Arum away. Catch!' And she was gone, holding the mysterious something to her side. Lesley stumbled into her shoes and climbed over the fence to take a short cut through the calf paddocks. She began to run, seeing the golden hump that was Sharon lying down in the bottom end of the paddock.

'She's seen me coming, she's getting up. May as well stop running. (Puff!) Nearly dead (puff) from exhaustion anyway. If only she hasn't calved!'

Sharon hadn't calved; in fact she didn't get round to it until much later in the evening, after David and Val had milked and Lesley had fed the nine winter calves; after Ian had returned rather damp, but lamentably fishless, from fishing; after Mr Mitchell had mowed the Home and Clover Paddocks and Mrs Mitchell had concocted a delicious fresh salad for tea; and after Val and Lesley had discussed their afternoon's efforts towards what they called the Pony Project.

'Your story for the competition,' said Val in their first moment of privacy since dinner time. 'Have you finished it?'

They were in the bathroom together, washing off the grime so easily collected simply by spending one active day on a busy dairy farm.

'Yes,' said Lesley. 'But what was it you were doing in the stable all afternoon? I've been dying of curiosity since milking time.'

'Oh, that . . . I'll go and get it if you bring the story for me to read.' Val wrung out her shoulder-length hair over the bath, and Lesley thought how odd it was to see it loosed from its perpetual pigtails; rather like seeing a short-sighted person without his glasses. Then she wrapped the long wet strands of her own hair in a towel and padded after Val to the bedroom they shared.

Val got something down from the top of the bookcase and put it in her hands. 'It's a bark painting.'

'Gosh,' said Lesley eloquently, staring in wonder at what Val had made. 'But what's a bark painting when it's at home?'

'It's all made with bark stuck to the cardboard with glue. I saw an article in the *Women's Weekly* and got the bark down in the River Paddock. You wouldn't believe there'd be such a variety.'

'It's terrific,' said Lesley, and meant it. The cardboard was about six inches by eight and was covered with bark to represent a river bank with trees. The sky was creamy, thin bark, the river was thin strips of varying grey with stiff splinters for rushes. The bank had a reddish tinge receding to darker distant mountains, and the sturdy gum-trees were realistically topped with a scattering of bubbly bark that looked grey up close, but green from a distance. The whole thing was astonishingly effective; Lesley could hardly believe that it was all made of bark. 'Gorgeous,' she elaborated admiringly. 'Show me this marvellous article.'

They did a swap, the *Women's Weekly* for Lesley's story, and each read in silence for a few minutes.

'Um,' remarked Val noncommittally as she put down *Lost on Shale Hill*.

'Mm?' said Lesley hopefully.

'Pretty good, though I'm no literary critic. A bit too much of that descriptive guff for me, but the judges will probably go for it. I like the bit where they all fall into the river while the other bloke bolts with the vital bundle.'

Well, Val was not noted for her enthusiasm for anything literary, Lesley told herself firmly. 'I wish I could think of another way to earn money,' she sighed, taking the towel off her hair and getting started with a comb. 'I don't reckon I've much chance with this. Probably thousands of other entries. But your future's obviously cut out for you.'

'Huh?'

'Bark painting! Didn't you see where it says thirty and fifty dollars? And you don't need to buy anything but glue.'

'Yes, but look at the size of those paintings, compared with the female that made them. About three feet square,

I'd say. The pictures, I mean, not the female. It'd take weeks to do one that big, and the frame looks pretty expensive, too. Then I s'pose you'd have to put them in a shop, or perhaps a show, to be sold. Frightfully complicated.'

Lesley said that difficulties were made to be overcome, weren't they? And she reckoned very small ones would probably make good souvenirs.

A rude thumping on the door drowned the end of her remark, and Ian charged impatiently into their room.

'I've just been over to the Maternity Ward. Sharon's calving and Dad thought you might like to watch, Lesley, as you haven't seen a cow calving before.'

'I have,' said Val. 'Twice. It takes simply ages. And there's something else I want to do.'

But Lesley grabbed her windcheater and hauled it on over her pyjamas as she dashed out. Ian said he wasn't going back; there were cows calving all the time and he wanted to watch the Rolf Harris Special on television; so she ran out of the gate and down the track alone.

The Maternity Ward was a tiny paddock just opposite the dairy, handy for easy inspection of calving cows. Many of the Mitchell's cows calved quite happily out in the paddock with their herd mates around them, but occasionally things went wrong. Older cows sometimes got milk fever, a calving-time disease that paralysed the cow's hindquarters, making it difficult for her to have the calf and impossible for her to get up. It was easily cured with a calcium injection, so when calving was known to be imminent, Guara cows were confined in the Maternity Ward until it was all over. There was a warm shed with electric lighting, straw bedding, a hayrack, a pile of sacks for calf-drying in emergencies, and a high shelf with a row of calcium bottles and a needle. Lesley had seen the needle in use on a milk-fever case, and hated it, for all its magical cure. In all her twelve years, however, she had never seen a calf born; left to themselves, cows usually calved in the night in the most distant, most secluded places they could find.

The gate was open, but she stopped running and crept round the corner of the shed to peer through the doorway. The electric light was on against the gathering dusk, and Sharon was prostrate on the floor with Mr Mitchell and David in attendance. That is, they were propping up the wall of the shed and talking quietly together, looking quite remarkably casual, thought Lesley, in view of what was happening right before their eyes. They both turned to smile at Lesley as she came in, remarking respectively, 'Just in time, dear,' and, 'Fetching combination, windcheater and pyjamas!' but she hardly heard, gazing at the cow and taking in the rhythmic contractions, the laboured breathing, and the tiny pair of yellowy hooves that had already appeared as a result.

'Coming on nicely,' remarked Mr Mitchell, 'but the head must be a bit tight.' He knelt down behind the cow and carefully grasped the slippery hooves, pulling gently but steadily when she pushed; and presently a black muzzle appeared, resting neatly on the front legs. The calf's head was 'a bit tight', and by the time it popped out a long pink tongue had appeared too, protruding from the clammy mouth and wavering hopefully. The head was the broadest part of the calf. Immediately after it appeared, there was a quick slither as the long, slender body slipped out and then it was all over. There on the straw was the calf, already snuffling and flapping its ears and trying to lift its head. Lesley stared in delight as Sharon lumbered to her feet with a quick grunt and began to lick her baby, uttering urgent, loving moos in between sturdy rasps with her tongue.

Mr Mitchell straightened up. 'A bull,' he announced, 'And I'm glad, really. She was our top cow last year – he should make a good breeder.' He wiped his hands on one of the sacks and David went out to fill a bucket for Sharon. She drank two or three gallons in great, sucking gulps, then returned to the task of drying her son, occasionally looking anxiously over his damp, curly head at the three intruders.

'No sign of milk fever,' said Mr Mitchell with satisfaction. 'She'll get on better if we leave her to it for a while.' He glanced at his watch as David swung the door shut. 'Half past eight. Come on, Les. We'll be in time to see Rolf Harris after all!'

4 Moonlight – and inspiration

Lesley sat up in bed and tugged at her bedspread till it loosened and fell to the floor. Then the top blanket. She would have removed both blankets, retaining just the sheet, but knew that if she did, she would probably wake up shivering before morning. If she ever succeeded in getting to sleep, that was. She thumped the pillow into shape and lay down with a sigh of frustration. Here it was, well past ten o'clock, with a hundred jobs to help with before early church the next morning, and for some reason she couldn't sleep. Perhaps it was the oppressive heat, or maybe worry about Arum. The pony had looked quite safe behind her repaired fence at bedtime. If they had shut her in the stable she would have kicked the wall all night; but what if she did manage to escape and damage something before morning? She might be sold before the competition entry was even posted, before anyone else even saw Val's beautiful bark painting. Lesley rolled over and glared resentfully across the room at the dim hump that was Val, fast asleep. How dare she sleep so soundly when she, Lesley, was still wide-awake and burdened with all the worries in the world? It was unkind, unfair, indecent! Lesley reached for the handkerchief under the pillow and blew her nose. Mum had said she'd probably get a cold, rushing out to see the calf again in her pyjamas. As if you got colds in summer, Lesley thought indignantly, and blew her nose again. But even if she did, it would be worth it for that walk into the cool summer night with her father to check up on Sharon before going to bed.

It had been so stifling in the maternity shed that Mr Mitchell had opened the door and carried the well-dried bull calf out to the paddock. Sharon had followed at his elbow, mooing desperately, so anxious for her son that when he was put down she nearly knocked him over with her motherly nudges and licks. But the little bull had braced himself sturdily, getting the feel of his gangly legs and blundering around after the vital sustenance instinct told him was somewhere near.

First, he had investigated his mother's front legs. They seemed promising, but all he could find was brisket. So he had stumbled down to the other end. More promising still, with that fragrant, milky smell, but every time he probed for a teat he moved out of licking range, and his mother would swing herself round to carry on the good work. This, of course, moved her udder out of probing range, so the calf would have to take four wobbly steps to reach it again, and the whole tiresome process would be repeated. Finally, however, they had reached a compromise: the little bull standing head-to-tail with his mother and sucking energetically at her front teat, and Sharon with her neck bent right round so that she could just reach to lick his tail whenever its enthusiastic wiggling brought it into range.

Lesley had been much amused at this performance, and so impressed with the calf's quick progress that she had chattered constantly about him to Val at bedtime. But Val had drifted off to sleep as usual and Lesley had stopped thinking about the calf and begun to think about the story she had written; she must make sure her entry was the best effort she was capable of producing.

The calf . . . the competition. She must have been getting a bit drowsy, for at this point the two subjects began to merge together, and she became aware of a glimmer in her mind which had something to do with both of them. The idea that spurred her back to wakefulness was an inspiration of something to write about Sharon's calf. Something that would do for the competition if she could just find a pencil and paper – quickly, before it was gone.

She was out of bed, rummaging in a desk drawer by moonlight. The moon was very bright tonight, bright enough to write by. She scribbled urgently, while the glimmer stayed in her mind and the memory of the evening was still fresh. The idea was clear-cut and the rhymes easy to find, and just a few minutes later she wrote the title above her poem – *The Newborn Calf*, and read it through.

The first thing he sees is his mother's shape
Against the dusky evening sky.
The first thing he hears is her tender call
As she answers his quavering baby cry.

The first thing he feels is her loving tongue
Rasping over his shivering skin.
The first thing he does is struggle to rise,
An age-old instinct urging him.

The first thing he tastes is his mother's milk,
Warm and vital to make him strong.
The first thing he knows is a mother's care
As she keeps her vigil all night long.

(Of course she wouldn't. She'd either go to sleep or get milk fever, but the vigil bit sounded right; it was poetic licence, anyway.)

Lesley put away the paper and got into bed again, but she was still restless. The moonlight was terribly bright. Perhaps that was what was keeping her awake. She arose once more, and gingerly lowered the creaking blind they hardly ever used. The bedroom was plunged into darkness so complete that she had to feel her way cautiously back to bed. Five minutes later, she was asleep.

5 Monday

Monday morning was one frantic rush for all the family except Mr Mitchell, who, apart from milking and dining as usual, planned to spend the day on the tractor mowing the Ten Acre Paddock, alternately stripping down to just shorts and boots, and hastily covering up again when his back began to get sunburnt.

Sharon had gone down with milk fever the night before, so her son had been taken away and tied up in the barn, and the job of teaching him to drink was one more addition to the Monday morning rush. Mrs Mitchell had accomplished this task with an old wine bottle and a rubber teat before hurrying inside to cut school lunches. Val and Lesley had fed the nine winter calves, who, despite the fact that they were four months old, still got milk every morning because they were pedigreed building blocks for the new stud, and Mr Mitchell wanted to give them a good start in life. David had helped milk, as usual, and Ian's contribution was the same every morning – running or riding Arum out to collect the newspaper from the mail-box at the boundary fence.

As all these jobs were finished at different times, breakfast was a rather chaotic affair eaten in relays, with people dashing all over the kitchen rounding up cornflakes and milk, under-boiling eggs, burning toast, spilling coffee, and saying loudly at intervals, 'Who's pinched the sugar?', 'That was *my* toast!' or, 'No tomato sandwiches for me, please, Mum, they go all soggy,' while Mrs Mitchell stood at the sink packing lunch-boxes with a high degree of efficiency due to years of practice.

Agonized glances at the clock, frustrated searches for lost ties and homework, suspected skimping of teeth-cleaning, and usually four individual slammings of the door: all these things their mother had come to expect and managed to cope with on an ordinary school morning. Still, there was no denying it was pleasant to sit down and get herself some breakfast when they were gone. There was usually time to talk things over quietly with Jim, and perhaps read the paper before tackling the housework.

Miraculously, they all caught the bus which dropped Ian off at the Primary School a mile away before taking the others on to the District High School. David and Val were arguing about whose watch was giving the right time, but Lesley, who didn't own a watch, sat in silence and wondered when, during a busy school day, she would have an opportunity to post her letter, which had only a few days to get to Hobart. She had spent part of Sunday afternoon copying out *Lost on Shale Hill* and *The Newborn Calf* in her best handwriting for the competition. Her parents didn't know about either entry, and she hadn't shown the poem to Val, somehow fearing the opinion of her more forthright and practical sister. Val was definitely not poetical – though, oddly enough, she was really quite artistic in a sensible sort of way. Her bark paintings were really very impressive. This morning Ian had come in from putting Arum's bridle away demanding to know who on earth had left bits of bark all over the stable bench. Since it was impossible to ignore him, Val had pleaded guilty and produced by way of explanation her bark-painting efforts, which now numbered two. They had been exclaimed over and greatly admired by everyone, especially Mrs Mitchell, who had turned a couple of old prints out of their frames so that the bark pictures could be displayed in style, hung proudly over the mantelpiece.

In the lunch break, Lesley seized her chance and dashed unlawfully off the school grounds to drop her letter in a mail-box. For some reason, now it was posted, her anxieties about Arum crowded back, and she was preoccupied all afternoon. Really, everything was going well. Her father had passed no more remarks on the state of the Home Paddock where Arum had broken in, and Arum herself had behaved impeccably for two whole days, spending the daytime tied in the lanes to clear up the long summer grass, and nights back in the Pony Paddock, where she could talk through the still upstanding fence to Valleywood Gipsy and Co, with whom she had struck up quite a friendship.

But there was still the nuisance of sharing her with two other active riders, and somehow, now the Pony Project had been started, this arrangement irked Lesley more than it had before. She found herself daydreaming about the Other Pony, who would be beautiful, intelligent, well-mannered and her very own, the exact opposite of poor darling Arum in every way. A couple of years ago, in the same situation, Lesley would just have written PONY hopefully on her Christmas list, as Ian was inclined to do, but now she had the beginnings of a responsibility he didn't have, and wouldn't have dreamed of making such a futile suggestion to her parents. She didn't really understand the family's financial situation, and didn't like to ask about it, but she realized that, though there was no cause for alarm (hadn't her father just purchased six expensive heifers?) it was not easy to make a good living on a small farm these days, and she also gathered that in order to do so, a good deal of capital had to be invested for good buildings, efficient machinery and high-quality animals.

Fortunately for Lesley, it was the last week of the school year, and since nothing very important was going on now that exams were over, her inattention was not noticed. Despite its being the last week, however, homework was still being set for some of the older students, as Lesley discovered when she joined Val and David in the bus queue at the end of the day.

'It's just not fair!' Val was complaining bitterly as she sorted out her books on the bus. 'Everybody else is getting quite human now we've done our exams. Christmas cheer coming up; peace in school, goodwill towards students all over the place, and what does Old Hammer go and do?'

'Give up. Who's Old Hammer, anyway?'

'You know, Les. Miss Nailor, Social Studies. Shocking case of over-enthusiasm. Just wait till you get her next year. Unless some praiseworthy type laces her coffee with arsenic before then.'

'What *has* she done?' asked David, on his way to the front of the bus as the Mitchells' stop approached.

Val pushed after him, but couldn't get close enough to carry on the conversation until after the bus dumped them at the turn-off to the farm.

'Dished out a whacking great dose of homework, that's what she's done! Says she wants to round off a good year's work and sets some reading, then says one of the maps in my notebook isn't up to standard and would I kindly do it again, Valerie.'

'Terrible,' said David unsympathetically. 'I wonder how Dad's getting on with the mowing.'

'Your guess is nearer than mine. Then she announces she wants it turned in tomorrow, and Social Studies is my first period!'

'We Leavers aren't having periods any more. I reckon I might get out of the rest of the week altogether if we start baling before school breaks up.'

'Lucky animal.' Val began complaining again, but Lesley had stopped listening. It was terribly hot, especially for her feet in their regulation grey socks and black shoes, and she was practically counting the steps till she was home and could take them off, take the whole dreary uniform off and perhaps have time for a swim before milking and tea.

Between the town and Guara, the land on either side of the road belonged to Turners, the Mitchells' neighbours, who also bred Jerseys. After half a mile of Turners' paddocks, there was a solid post-and-rail boundary fence joined by a gate across the road. It was always a relief to reach the boundary gate and know they were nearly home, and on days like these it was doubly pleasant, for the single enormous gum-tree on the Mitchells' side of the gate-post threw at least ten yards of the road into delicious cooling shade. It was an awesome and magnificent tree, the only gum on the whole willow-and-ti-tree property, and it was because of this tree that the Mitchells called their place Guara – an Aboriginal word for gum-tree. This as where the mailbox was (for deliveries would come no farther), and also where the proud new sign: GUARA JERSEY STUD – J. R. MITCHELL had been nailed to the tree itself. Lesley looked at it with a vague but pleasant sensation of welcome and belonging. David looked at it and thought that soon it would be 'J. R. MITCHELL AND SON', and Val looked at it and stopped grumbling long enough to think, as she always did, that it was very badly designed and she could have done much better lettering herself.

Ian, who had arrived home from school half an hour

earlier, met his brother and sisters at the front gate, and began talking before they were even in earshot, so that they only caught the last bit of what he was saying:

'... I simply tore home to go swimming with the other kids, then I got trapped and now they'll have gone without me.'

'Trapped?' asked David, visualizing half a dozen terrible things that could have happened on the farm.

'In the kitchen, by Auntie Joy. She parked her car round the corner in the shade, so I didn't see it and barged straight in. She's in there now, talking to Mum. I wouldn't go in there for anything if I were you lot.'

David said thanks for the warning; he had a pair of overalls in the dairy he could change into for milking, and he promptly departed. Val was clearly thinking along the same lines, but Lesley opened the gate, saying she was simply dying of hunger, and Auntie Joy wasn't a bad old stick, anyway.

'At a distance,' muttered Val. 'Say, about fifty miles!' but she followed Lesley in through the back door and they managed to fight down hunger pains long enough to get changed before heading for the kitchen.

'Oh, hullo, Auntie Joy!' Well-simulated surprise. Being greeted gushingly and soundly kissed on the cheek. Enduring small talk for a decent interval before raiding the fridge and biscuit-tin. Val trying to remember what colour Auntie Joy's hair had been last time (she thought ash-blonde but now it was a blue rinse), and Lesley wondering for the hundredth time how two women so totally dissimilar as Auntie Joy and their mother could possibly be sisters.

'Where's David?' Mrs Mitchell asked suspiciously. Lesley hastily replied that he had gone straight on to milk, '— as Dad's still mowing, you know.'

But Auntie Joy didn't even hear. She was saying enthusiastically to Val, 'I've just been admiring your bark pictures, dear. Nancy tells me no one even taught you how to do them. I think they're just lovely. I wanted to buy one, but Mum wouldn't hear of it, so I thought you might make one for me. And perhaps a couple more to give away. They'd make *such* unusual Christmas presents. And of course you can put a good price on these handmade things. Oh, dear, I shouldn't have said that, should I? Never mind, perhaps you'll make a special concession to Aunties!'

Val leaned against the kitchen door with a polite smile, chewing mechanically at a biscuit and not really absorbing anything until she caught the word 'price' and the penny dropped. She glanced across at Lesley and knew they were both thinking the same thing – Pony Project. She promptly swapped her polite smile for an interested one and really listened as her aunt rambled on happily about framing and souvenirs. When she finally got round to placing a definite order for one large painting and two small ones, by Christmas, Val thought she had heard enough, and seized on a rare pause while Auntie Joy was drinking her tea to recite the well-planned piece she had been rehearsing to herself for several minutes.

'I'm afraid I'll have to go now, Auntie. Old H —, Miss Nailor, set us some homework, rather a lot, and I've got to finish it for tomorrow morning. But I'll get your paintings done as soon as I can, and post them down to you.'

Auntie Joy put down her cup. 'Don't worry about me, dear, I daresay I'll be up this way again before Christmas. Burnie is getting so crowded it's almost a relief to get out into the country.'

Val and Lesley grabbed another biscuit each and bolted.

'Twenty minutes,' said Val, looking at her watch. 'We did better than old Ian. It took him half an hour to get out. Phew!' she added, collapsing at her desk and poking around for books, 'I'm almost grateful to Old Hammer and her perishing homework.'

'Don't be beastly,' said Lesley reprovingly. 'This is the first proper chance we've had for making money and that's all you can say.'

'Oh, I'm grateful all right, in a way, but it's so hard to do the right thing in the face of all that energetic gushing. Now, where's the atlas?'

Lesley found it for her, then asked, a little tentatively, 'Do you mind if I have a go at bark painting? After all, it's really my pony we're saving for, as you said.'

'Heavens, no. It's pretty easy, really. There's a bag of assorted bark concealed under my bed, but you'll have to find your own glue and stuff.'

Lesley found these, and settled down opposite Val, who was busily tracing the outline of the British Isles with a blue pencil. With several references to the *Women's Weekly* article, she cut out a modest square of thick cardboard and sketched a simple landscape on it, just a road, a tree, and mountains in the distance. Now, the sky. But the glue seemed terribly thick, and the light bits of bark meant to represent the sky kept sticking to her fingers instead of the cardboard. It was an erratic-looking sky when she had finished, highly suggestive of a storm, so she decided to give the tree a wind-tossed effect to be in keeping. But the tree wasn't shaping well, and when she tried to pick bits of it up to move them over, the sky and mountains underneath lifted too. She dabbed on in silent frustration that was presently broken by an anguished wail from Val, who crumpled up her map and hurled it into the wastepaper-basket.

'I *thought* the British had sprouted a few extra Isles since I last looked! But now I find they're potatoes!' Seeing Lesley's blank face at this mystifying remark, she shoved over the atlas to show her. 'The trouble is, my tracing paper's so thick I could only just see the outline. So I just traced round the heavy black bits and it looked the right shape till I found I was going round all these extra islands. So I lifted up the tracing paper, and – see these little pictures of the Products, sheep and steel and so on, I'd been tracing round these *potatoes* out in the Irish Sea with arrows pointing to where they belong!' She laughed as Lesley grinned comprehendingly. 'I s'pose it is rather funny really. I'll show you.'

She scraped her stool away and bent down to rummage in the WPB but came up with two bits of paper and a peculiar expression.

'Have you been writing *poetry*, Les?' she said, in the same tone she might have used to enquire, 'Have you been smoking *pot*, Les?'

Lesley looked up guiltily and saw that her sister was reading the original copy of *The Newborn Calf*, which she remembered consigning to the basket the day before.

'Um,' said Val noncommittally, folding it up. 'For that competition, I s'pose?'

Lesley nodded warily.

'Um,' said Val thoughtfully, scratching her chin with it. 'I rather like it. But I wouldn't be too hopeful, Les. I mean, anything with rhymes and metres is hopelessly out of date these days. You should see the garbage we have to study in English. Long lines, half-finished sentences, weird ideas, and figurative language that doesn't figure at all. And rhymes just aren't in at the moment.' She paused. 'But I like it . . . How's your painting going?'

Lesley sighed and began clearing bits of bark off the

desk. 'No good at all. Look! It obviously takes something I was born without.'

Val took the cardboard square and turned it round several times. 'Which way up?' she asked in such honest perplexity that Lesley laughed and felt better.

'Never mind,' she said, dumping it in the WPB on top of the Irish Sea Potatoes. 'It's high time we fed Sharon's calf. Did you know Dad wants to call him Guara Supreme?'

'Yes, so David said. A bit high-sounding at the moment, but no doubt he'll grow up to it. I wonder if Auntie Joy's gone yet?'

6 Quite a useful jumper

By the end of the week the harvest was in full swing. Thursday evening found all the young Mitchells in the Home Paddock helping or hindering in various ways.

Favourable weather had dried the cut grass quickly and Mr Mitchell had raked it the previous day. He was now in the middle of the paddock driving the tractor, behind which the ancient press was slowly forking in the last of the grass at one end and coughing it out at the other as compact, compressed bales of hay, securely bound by green twine. Sometimes the secure bindings burst when a bale hit the ground, and sometimes a fault in the dark interior of the press sent out two bales bound together with the same length of twine, but apart from minor incidents like these everything was really going very well, and so far nothing had broken down.

As the tractor could hardly pull its trailer at the same time as the press, the land-rover was being used to cart the hay from paddock to barn. When the baling was well under way, David had begun driving it slowly along the uneven line of expelled bales, stopping every few yards for a bale to be hauled aboard by one of the two town men who comprised the 'extra labour'. One of these was a cheerful young student, Bruce Edwards, who liked to do part-time jobs such as this because, he said, it was good for his muscles, excellent for his bank balance, and as far removed from studying as anything he could think of. The other, one 'Smiler' Hodgets, was a tall, thin, lugubrious individual who took on over-time jobs because he had a worried little wife and nine disreputable children to support. Smiler's mournful features were set in a mould of perpetual gloom; during three harvests with the Mitchells, his only contribution to any conversation going had been to remark that it would 'rain tonight, for sure'.

Val and Lesley and Ian had been given the job of preparing the barn for hay storage. This meant clearing out everything from miscellaneous tools and building materials to Guara Supreme and a tiny heifer that had been born on Monday night and subsequently named Fiona. As both calves were drinking well, they had been turned out into the top calf paddock, where they executed a freedom gallop similar to that of the Valleywood heifers. With the barn looking unusually empty and tidy, Ian had departed to pester David to let him drive the land-rover, but Val and Lesley had saddled Arum and taken her to join the workers in the Home Paddock.

One of Arum's good points was her jumping ability, which had been developed both through escaping and schooling till she was quite a useful jumper. Val had discovered one year that it was great fun to jump hay bales, and since then it had become almost traditional to let Arum into the fun every harvest time. Another of her good points was that she was not adverse to machinery, even loud and unusual machinery like a hay press, so while everyone else worked like slaves Lesley and Val took turns at arranging groups of bales and jumping Arum round them. Bales in stacks instead of bales every ten yards were looked upon with favour by David, Bruce and Smiler, but their efforts to pick up the stacks were viewed with disfavour by Val and Lesley and also Ian, who soon gave up pestering David to join in the fun.

'It took Les and me ages to put up this triple!' he yelled above the noise of tractor, land-rover and press. 'And I haven't even had my turn at jumping over it yet. You go down the bottom end; there are plenty of loose bales down there we don't want!'

Smiler went on saying nothing as usual, but David and Bruce more or less obligingly took themselves and the land-rover down to the bottom end of the paddock to pick up bales there.

'But we'll have to come back here when we've unloaded this lot,' David yelled back. 'You've got about twenty minutes.'

Val cantered up and reluctantly relinquished Arum to Ian. 'Terrific!' she said to Lesley, collapsing on to a bale. 'She went beautifully, especially over the triple. Look, she's even going well for Ian!'

Lesley looked, and it was true. Arum, despite her poor conformation and outlandish gaits, looked quite different jumping, and her bright eyes and pricked arum-lily ears gave her an almost intelligent expression. 'It's like seeing Smiler Hodgets looking cheerful!' Lesley exclaimed. 'She's really enjoying herself. I couldn't bear to have her sold.'

'Trust you to drag in an unpleasant subject,' grumbled Val. 'Talking of unpleasant subjects,' she sighed, 'I really ought to be working on those darn bark paintings Bruce ordered for his mother.'

'That's not unpleasant, it's jolly optimistic,' Lesley objected.

'Not for me, it's not. *You* don't have to spend your summer holidays sitting inside making the darn things. It's all Mum's fault. If she hadn't had the men inside for cool drinks this afternoon, Bruce would never have seen them.'

'But she did, and he did, and he ordered a pair for his mother's birthday. That's four dollars, and another eight for the three you sold Auntie Joy. Twelve dollars altogether for the Pony Project.'

'Not quite – you've got to subtract the price of the frames,' Val pointed out. That comes to nearly three dollars. Frames are ruinous, even from the supermarket. Oh, dash!' she added, seeing the empty land-rover returning from the barn. 'Here they come for our jumps, and Ian hasn't even finished yet. We won't have time for another round.'

Lesley got up from her bale, eyeing the land-rover with disgust.

'Oh, well' – Val patted Arum's nose as Ian rode up and dismounted – 'she's getting pretty hot, and this is only the first paddock. There's always tomorrow, and the Clover Paddock's even bigger!'

Lesley took Arum's bridle, but as she turned to lead her away, David called out from where he had stopped the land-rover to pick up the bales in the first jump.

'Hoy! Mum wants you girls to run up and give her a hand with the grub. And please get a move on. We need it in a hurry!'

Lesley waved to show she had understood. She was very hungry herself, and even more thirsty, so she could imagine how the men felt. 'Hey, Ian! Let Arum go, will you? We've got to go in and help Mum.'

Ian caught the reins flung to him and stared after his departing sisters in disgust. Fancy getting Arum out like that and expecting him to put her away! Serve 'em right if he just left her there. But he couldn't very well do that, not in the middle of all this machinery. And he s'posed he *had* taken his turn at jumping her. Still, there was no point in slogging all the way up the paddock on foot. He passed Arum's reins over her head and scrambled into the saddle.

'Grub' turned out to be a great stack of sandwiches, dark, moist chunks of fruit cake and milk-shakes all round. Everyone stopped work gratefully. It was a very humid, breathless evening and there were still two or three loads to be carted in, though the baler had finished its work in the Home Paddock. The sandwich stack diminished rapidly and the fruit cake seemed to vanish into thin air. Everyone came back for second milk-shakes except Mrs Mitchell and Lesley, who knew that if the two big jugs were emptied she would most likely be the one sent back for refills. David and his father cheerfully discussed the quality and quantity of the hay the paddock had yielded; Bruce and Mrs Mitchell cheerfully discussed the mess modern education was in; and Smiler chomped away at a hunk of fruit cake and remarked that it was far too humid tonight, far too sticky – it's rain before Sat'dee for sure.

Lesley helped stack the tumblers and went up to the house with her mother to help wash them up, too, but Val was delighted to be invited to drive the land-rover for the last loads. When Lesley returned, reluctant to miss anything, she found Val at the wheel with her father, David, Bruce and Smiler all collecting and stacking bales and Ian on top of the load, teetering perilously and occasionally getting a bale dropped on his feet. Since the bales were much too heavy for her to lift, she joined Val in the cab, sniffing appreciatively its unique farmlike aroma. Suddenly Val's voice penetrated her straying thoughts.

' . . . just clutch, brake and accelerator. It's frightfully simple, and of course any mug can steer.'

'What?'

'You weren't listening! I was saying that this is all very well, but I've got to finish those paintings, so do you think you could drive? It's all low gear, just stopping and starting, really, for each bale. If I put the hand-accelerator on you've only got to use the clutch, not even the brake on the flats like this.'

'Do you think Dad will let me?'

'Dad wouldn't mind anything except Ian at the controls! He knows more about it, but you're not nearly as reckless. Look, I'll put the hand-accelerator on and we can change over in motion.'

They did, and Lesley found herself awesomely in complete control of the land-rover. It was really very simple, she discovered, though she had to concentrate hard to do what an experienced driver would have done by reflex action.

'And of course you don't have to drive anywhere but in the paddock,' Val was saying. 'Dad or David always take over at the gate to back into the barn. O.K.? I shall betake myself to the bark!' she announced dramatically, and got out at the next stop.

Lesley heard a brief argument which resulted in Ian going home with her, as it was nine o'clock and Mrs Mitchell didn't want everyone in the bathroom at once. 'But it's really only eight o'clock,' she heard him disputing, 'if you look at it from a daylight saving point of view.' Daylight saving or not, dusk was gathering fast now, and at the next stop David came to turn on the headlights for her.

'Last load,' he said encouragingly. 'I'll take over when we've picked up these few in the middle.'

As she lifted her foot from the clutch again, Lesley realized that she was driving automatically now. It was really quite like learning to ride a horse. 'Only a horse has the sense to stop when it sees a wall or a cliff edge,' she thought, 'whereas with a vehicle it's entirely up to you.'

With the last load from the Home Paddock stacked in the barn, Bruce and Smiler went home, one riding a bicycle and calling out to Lesley to hurry her sister along with his mother's birthday present; the other rattling off in a battered utility after arranging to come back after work the next day, if it wasn't raining.

'I'll just nip over to Maternity and check up on Maria,' said Mr Mitchell. 'You kids go on in. It's pretty late and you'll be busy tomorrow.'

David and Lesley headed wearily towards the lighted house, only deviating for a moment to check on the two baby calves.

'Supreme will be a breeding bull for us one day,' David said. 'Fiona's a nice little heifer, but she can't be registered.'

'Why not?'

'Because her mother's a grade, an unregistered cow. You can't register calves from grade cows, even if they're pure Jersey and by a registered bull. But Sharon's one of the first registered cows we bought, and Dad's already registered Supreme with the Jersey Herd Society, so he's entitled to a full pedigree and stud name and everything.'

'How complicated,' said Lesley, frowning as she tried to absorb this. 'Why are pedigreed cows better than ordinary cows?'

'Some of them aren't,' replied David, grinning. 'A pedigree's not a guarantee or anything, it's just a complete record of how an animal is bred. Like writing down formulae in science. When you get a good cow, you study her bloodlines (the recipe she was made from, so to speak) and you study up genetics and hereditary tendencies if you're keen enough, then you try to breed even better cows. Most grade men don't care about breeding as long as they get their cows in calf regularly. They miss out on all that interest.'

'Do you really find it all that interesting?'

'Of course! It's what I've always wanted to do, stay on the farm and breed cattle.' He hesitated. 'I sometimes think I'd have liked to go to an agricultural college, but in a way I'm glad it's impossible, as I can get started so much sooner. Especially with the Valleywood heifers. It always pays to start a stud with the very best foundation stock you can.'

'What a pity they're only yearlings,' said Lesley. 'We'll have to wait a whole year till they have calves and come in milk.'

They both paused at the garden gate to glance at the heifers in the Bottom Calf Paddock: and they both saw the same thing at the same moment. Mr Mitchell, coming back from the Maternity Ward, caught up with them in time to see their exchanged glances of comical horror.

'What's up?' he called. 'You should be inside.'

'Arum!' said Lesley expressionlessly, pointing.

Her father peered through the dim shadows, partly blinded by the house lights, and saw what they saw. Arum Lily, calmly grazing in the middle of the Bottom Calf Paddock, surrounded by a curious bunch of Valleywood heifers.

'Ian put her away all right. She must have just leaned on the fence then jumped it, after all that practice over bales tonight.' Lesley glanced apologetically, almost fearfully, at her father, but Mr Mitchell said indulgently, 'Leave her for now. Let her have a decent feed. There's more than enough there for those six heifers. You or Val can get her out in the morning.'

'And whip up a few more of those famous tourniquets for her fence,' said David drily.

Lesley sighed with relief and yawned, then yawned again. In a hazy dream of exhaustion she kicked off her shoes and followed the menfolk inside.

'Hurry up, darling,' her mother greeted her. 'You'll have to use the same bathwater as Val, and she's nearly finished.

Bathing in lukewarm water. Drying slowly and putting on her lightest pair of pyjamas. Opening wide the bedroom windows and leaving her top blanket off. Another milkshake. Distant sounds from the television as she cleaned her teeth. Fumbling drowsily into bed without turning the light on. Val's bed creaking as she turned over, but nothing could prevent Lesley getting to sleep tonight. Nothing . . .

7 Moonlight – and desperation

Nothing did, but Lesley was awakened a few hours later by a sound outside the open window. Visitors? she wondered hazily. Surely not at this hour. She rolled over lethargically and strained to see the luminous dial of their bedroom clock. Twenty past twelve. And there it was again. A clacking sound, like high heels on the concrete path. But there were no lights, no voices. A little nervous, Lesley sat up in bed and peered out fearfully into the moonlight. A dark moving shape on the lawn caused her to stiffen with momentary terror, but a second later she recognized it for what it was. A cow. She got out of bed, trying to remember which paddock the cows should be in. Surely the Creek Paddock, at night, but if so, how could they possibly have found their way into the garden? A second shape loomed, larger and more angular than the first. Arum! With a shock, Lesley realized that they were not cows in the garden, but heifers, the Valleywood heifers, and somehow it was all Arum's fault.

Suddenly the garden seemed full of heifers, and there was that high-heeled noise again, the clacking sound of dainty hooves on the concrete. She hoped no one else had heard it, especially her father. The consequences would be too awful even to think of. Filled with apprehension now, she left the window and went over to tug at Val's motionless shoulder.

'Val,' she whispered, 'wake up! Quickly!'

Val stirred reluctantly and opened one eye. 'Whassup?'

she inquired sleepily, then roused a little on sensing Lesley's urgency.

'Hurry up! Arum's let the heifers out somehow, and now they're all wandering round the garden.'

'Gosh!' Val got up to look. One glance was enough, and she was slipping her feet into thongs. 'But how could Arum possibly have done it? She was O.K. when I came in.'

'When *I* came in she was in the Bottom Calf Paddock with the heifers. Dad saw her too, but he said to leave her there till morning.'

'Did he? Must have been in a good mood! Get some shoes on quickly. We've got to get 'em out before they eat the roses. And think of the mess on the lawn.'

'Sssh! if we wake anyone up, poor old Arum's in the soup worse than ever.'

They crept down the silent hall and out through the back door, wincing every time a floor-board creaked.

'The main thing is to get them out of the garden,' Val whispered. 'Then we can see where they got out and get them back in again.' She closed the door inch by inch and they picked their way round the clothes-line to check the garage and woodshed. 'Both empty. Now we'd better go right round the house, collecting the heifers as we go, and drive them out into the lane.'

She dodged sideways to turn a heifer that loomed towards them out of the darkness, slipped, and measured her length on the ground. The heifer propped in alarm and promptly disappeared round the corner, lumbering into the lilac bush in her haste, and breaking off one of its branches with a resounding crack.

'Now you've done it,' groaned Lesley. 'What made you trip like that? It's not so terribly dark.'

Val picked herself up and investigated. 'Dung,' she said

disgustedly. 'Fresh, and in liberal quantities. Even if that row didn't wake everyone up, we're going to have a terrible time removing all traces!'

Lesley picked up the lilac branch and tossed it behind some bushes where it wouldn't be noticed. Immediately there was a shrill squeak, and two jet-propelled forms streaked across the lawn in front of her.

'W – what —?'

'Catkin and Possum,' said Val. 'You chucked half a lilac bush on them, you silly idiot! It only wants Tassel to start up now and we might as well have the Federal Band leading the way!'

Miraculously, in spite of everything, there were still no sounds or lights in the house as the girls made their way round it on to the front lawn. Here, as they had expected, were Arum and the heifers. What they had not anticipated was the whole lot advancing purposefully towards them at a good pace, not even pausing to sample Mrs Mitchell's roses.

'Gosh,' hissed Val, hitching up her pyjamas. 'Head 'em off, Les, or we'll be back where we started.'

Lesley stepped obediently into the breach, waving her arms, then glimpsed a silent upright figure behind the ghostly forms of the heifers and clutched her sister in terror.

'V-Val, there's someone behind them, driving them towards us!'

'Nonsense,' said Val sturdily, determined to be practical if it killed her. 'Whoever would want to do that? It must have been a branch you saw. Each an insane homicidal burglar couldn't possible have any reason . . . Look out, Les! They'll break away!'

A little steadied by her sister's common sense, Lesley took herself firmly in hand and moved in on the heifers, brandishing a stick. In the face of such determined tactics, the heifers and Arum soon retreated in the right direction, but this time it was Val who paused.

'What —?' began Lesley, then she heard it too. Footsteps that weren't hooves, a subdued 'Blast!' and the sudden appearance of a pyjama-clad figure in front of them.

'Lesley! Val!'

'DAVID! What on earth are you doing?'

They all realised the absurdity of the question as she asked it, but David sighed and answered anyway.

'The same as you, I think, but from a different direction! Trying to get these something heifers and that *something* HORSE out of here before they reduce the garden to ruins. Look, you two stay behind them and I'll nip over the fence to head them back in the right direction as they go through the gate.'

There was no time for parleying. The heifers and Arum were already gathering speed; their pounding hooves sounded thunderous to the three who so urgently desired silence. David only just gained enough lead to head them all off towards the calf paddocks as they trotted out of the front gate. Fortunately the heifers, at least, knew where they belonged, and made straight for the lane that led to the Bottom Calf Paddock. As the young Mitchells had expected, the gate was open, and they could see the dark shapes of the heifers streaming through. But Arum didn't follow. Lesley caught her by the forelock as she paused uncertainly. They walked after the heifers in silence. There was enough moonlight to see that the gate was not properly opened, just unfastened and dropped across the gateway.

'Same type of gate as the orchard one,' said David soberly, 'only no nail on this one, so she just nosed it open and let them all out.'

'David, don't tell Dad, please!' Lesley burst out desperately. 'Poor old Arum, she's unpopular enough as it is.'

'What about all the mess in the garden? How are you going to explain hoofmarks and dungpats and chewed flowers all over the place?'

'I'll clean it up before I go back to bed,' Lesley promised recklessly. '*Please*, Dave!'

'Just a minute,' Val interrupted as David bent to pick up the gate. 'Where can we put Arum?'

'Oh. I see. If we put her in the stable or somewhere, everyone will ask why.'

'And if we put her back where she should be, she'll repeat the whole performance.'

'Not if we make the gate pony-proof,' said David. 'Can't start bashing nails in at this hour, but I can tie the dropper to the post.'

Lesley led Arum into the lane while Val ran to get some of last year's binder twine from the barn. David shut the gate, then bound it securely to the straining post with several lengths of green twine.

'There are two other gates out of the Bottom Calf Paddock, so I s'pose I'd better fix them too,' he said resignedly. 'You two had better see what you can do in the garden, since you're so set on it. But Heaven help you if anyone wakes up. There's a shovel in the toolshed,' he added helpfully, and departed down the moonlight lane.

'I suppose,' grunted Val, scraping up dungpats from the lawn and shovelling them on to the garden, 'there'll come a time – where's the one I slipped on? – we'll laugh about tonight, but at the moment' (grunt) 'I seriously doubt it.'

'Me too,' agreed Lesley feelingly. She was on hands and knees raking over the trampled flower-beds. 'Isn't it lucky it's a full moon? Fancy doing all this on a cold dark night by torchlight.'

'A dark night might have been too dark for Arum to jump her fence and open that gate,' said Val. 'I sometimes wonder if she's worth saving. And,' she continued determinedly to block Lesley's indignant protest, 'I'm beginning to wonder the same thing about our respective pyjamas, after me tripping in the dung and you kneeling in the dirt! But I do grant it's a good thing it's so dry – the hoof-prints on the lawn would be inches deep if it was winter.'

It was five past one by David's watch and a quarter past by Val's when the three of them finally crept back to bed that night, after washing dirty hands and feet under the garden tap. All exhaustion from the energetic day had vanished with the creeping urgency of the midnight drama, and Lesley now found it hard to sleep.

She woke after only a few hours' sleep, her mind filled with anxious thoughts about Arum and the condition of the garden. It was odd to look out on the sunbathed lawn as she dressed: the memory of the night's activities already had a faintly dreamlike quality. Lesley slipped into her thongs and went out quietly to make a brief sortie round the garden.

'Arum's still in with the heifers,' she reported thankfully to Val after her quick inspection. 'Mum's been down to feed the chooks already and I don't *think* she's noticed anything.'

Val pulled her shirt on over her head, to save unbuttoning, and looked out of their bedroom window.

'It's a mercy the ground's so hard. There would have been millions of footprints otherwise. I think our worst lookout is that lilac branch, but I s'pose one of us can confess to knocking that off by mistake, if necessary. Bring your pyjamas along and we can dump them quietly into the washing-machine on the way out.'

'There's the place where you tripped,' said Lesley as they went out the back gate, 'but I don't think anyone would notice that if they didn't know.'

Val yawned. 'I think we came out of it pretty well, except for lack of sleep.'

In the dairy a few minutes later, Lesley and Val looked up from collecting buckets and stirring calf milk as David came in from the cow-yard.

'You look a bit under the weather,' commented Val. 'Had a hard day's night?'

Lesley put down her buckets and said, 'We did a marvellous job last night. I checked this morning, but the garden's O.K. and no one's noticed a thing.'

David looked at them both gravely.

'I noticed something. Before milking. We must have put only five heifers back last night. There's one missing this morning; I'm afraid it's Gipsy.'

8 One missing heifer

Val stopped stirring the milk, appalled.

'Gipsy, the best one! Help, we'd better go looking for her right away! Or should we feed the calves first?'

A horrible thought came to Lesley. 'Does Dad know?'

'Not yet,' said David grimly. 'But if we can't find her before breakfast we'll have to tell him, of course. I've got to go back and help him with the cows now, but I had a quick look round before milking, and she's definitely not in her paddock, or the Pony Paddock. I think you two had better feed the cows double-quick, then get Ian and start looking.'

'But where could she be?' Lesley asked in consternation.

'You know what happened last night. Your guess is as good as mine. But I'd try the lanes, then the open hay paddocks, if I were you. And keep a look-out for tracks.'

He went back to the inner part of the dairy in response to a call from Mr Mitchell, and his sisters returned to their jobs in a flurry of urgency.

The nine winter calves were fed in record time that morning, and Supreme and Fiona, the babies, had their buckets whisked in and out so quickly that they hardly tasted the milk, and completely missed the petting and attention they normally received. Ian was hauled away from his guinea-pigs, and Val all but gagged him to stop his protests long enough to explain. Exasperatingly, when he finally comprehended the situation, he seemed more aggrieved at being left out of the night's fun than worried about Gipsy's disappearance and the possible consequences for Arum.

'She's bound to turn up, they always do. And I can't just leave Harry and George. They're starving hungry, and so am I.'

Val was infuriated, but she could never resist organizing people, so she said briskly, 'All right then. Feed the little so-and-sos and *hurry up*. Lesley can go and get Arum for searching the big paddocks and I'll sneak in and filch some grub to keep us all going.'

Ten minutes later, the three of them and Arum were assembled at the gateway to the calf paddocks, fortifying themselves with bananas and homemade biscuits.

'The first thing is to make sure there are no more possible outlets apart from this one,' began Val, and Lesley was sure, though it seemed incredible, that she was actually enjoying the emergency.

It didn't take long to check the little paddock. The other corner gates were firmly shut, and the fence was completely innocent of any suspiciously wide gaps or low slants.

'O.K.' said Val, feeding her banana-skin to Arum, who had refused the offer of a biscuit. 'She obviously came out of this gate with the rest of them, but somehow got separated. It's no use looking for tracks here where they all galloped through, so we'd better split up. Ian, you go out and get the paper as usual, but keep a good look-out for tracks on the road. Lesley can do the nearer, smaller paddocks, and I'll take Arum up past the dairy on to the cow lanes. David said the gates to all the hay paddocks are open, so I'll canter round the edges of them, too.'

Then, using the technique of all the best organizers, Val wheeled Arum and cantered away before her instructions could be disputed.

Ian grumbled as he turned down the farm road, but Lesley had no wish to do any disputing. Her reactions to any situation were usually slow, and as she was the kind of person who dithers in a crisis, she was glad to accept authority in such times.

David had already checked the Pony Paddock, but Lesley cut across it to have a look in the orchard before moving into the Swamp Paddock. It was here that Willow Creek, the backwater that joined the river in the Willow Paddock, narrowed and branched till it was no more than a series of ditches interspersed with spongy hillocks and lumps of tussocks and rushes. A promising place to search for a lost heifer, thought Lesley, especially if (horrible thought) she was bogged in a mud hole. The next mental step in this logic would be to suspect drowning, but fortunately Lesley didn't get that far, having nearly become bogged herself through trusting a solid-looking hump that turned out to be a heap of floating water weed. 'Good thing I'm wearing shorts,' she thought, hauling herself out of the thigh-deep, clinging mud. She looked down at her legs in distaste then decided to search the Willow Paddock as well, pausing to wade into the river to shorts-level and rub off the telltale mud in the clear flowing current. There was no trace of Gipsy in this area, much as she had expected, so she looked up in hopeful anticipation when Val hailed her from the River Paddock a few minutes later. Running across the cow pastures to join her, Lesley noticed that her sister was dismounted and trying to keep Arum away from something on the ground.

'Come and hang on to this animal,' called Val as soon as she was within earshot. 'There are some tracks here I'm trying to look at and she keeps blundering on top of them.'

Lesley obediently led Arum a little way off, and smiled as she watched Val kneel to examine the dust.

'You look just like the little boy looking for Alexander Beetle!'

Val straightened up and glared. 'You wait. I may soon look like the girl who found Valleywood Gipsy! I think they must be her tracks, and they're heading down towards the swimming-hole. Come on!'

Lesley followed with Arum at a cautious distance. But the willowy way down to the river soon became stony, and Val looked up, perplexed. 'They seem to peter out on the gravel. She could have gone in any direction from this point.'

'Ssh!' said Lesley, cocking her head and reaching out a hand to still Arum's jingling bridle. 'I think we're being hollered for.'

'Oh, heck! I suppose we're horribly late for breakfast. And not a thing to show for it unless Ian's found her, which seems unlikely with these tracks.' Val came back to Arum reluctantly. 'Here, your turn to ride. I'll give you a leg up.'

Ian had not found Gipsy, and in a quick, pre-breakfast conference David decided that their parents should be told without delay. It was a most inopportune time, with Mr Mitchell anxious to get on with his baling and annoyed because Ian was late with the newspaper, but it had to be done, so David waited till Ian's ticking-off was over, then broke the news.

'He was late because he was looking for Gipsy, Dad. We all were. I'm afraid she went missing sometime last night.'

Looking back, Lesley could never remember just what her father said then, or her mother, either. In fact, the whole ensuing conversation remained rather a blur in her mind, the sort of blur that you pushed down when it rose to the surface in order to keep yourself from the unpleasant experience of looking at it too clearly. The only bit she could recall was, 'Why didn't you tell me before?' and David's reply, 'Because we didn't want to give you any unnecessary worries on top of the harvest and everything' – but she knew the real reason was that David, too, had wanted to protect Arum if possible. She felt grateful, as well as mildly astonished, that he could be anything but totally loyal to the farm.

After a certain amount of deploring, reprimanding and explanation, the atmosphere cleared, and everybody began sensibly discussing what should be done. Val described the tracks she had seen, and Ian explained that he had found several hoofprints, including Arum's, near the dairy end of the road, but none going very far away, and no single spoor.

'Still, she could have kept going on the grass edges,' their father pointed out. 'I think I'll ring Turners first, and if they haven't seen anything we'll have a look at the tracks in the River Paddock.'

'David and I can look at Val's tracks,' his wife said firmly. 'It'll do me good to get outside for a bit, and you know you've got to have the Clover Paddock pressed before Bruce and Smiler get here.'

Val began to ask whether they thought she couldn't read tracks properly, or something, but her father got up and went to the telephone at this point, and Mrs Mitchell, hearing his disheartening side of the conversation with Mr Turner, began hurriedly clearing the table and washing up, urging everybody to help her.

'John hasn't seen any sign of her,' Mr Mitchell reported unnecessarily, 'so she's got to be still on the farm somewhere.'

'Unless she's got into the bush,' said David suddenly.

'Heaven forbid!' groaned Val. 'Fancy toiling up Shale Hill in this weather. The humidity would kill us even if the mosquitoes didn't!'

Her father frowned. 'It is much too humid. I'm afraid Smiler's right; we're in for a thunderstorm. You'd better have a good look at those tracks while you can.' He picked up his wide-brimmed hat and turned to go out. 'I'm in the Clover Paddock if anyone needs me.'

Lesley watched him go, feeling desperately sorry that he should have one worry after another crowding in at his busiest time of year. She knew just what it was like. She also knew that if Gipsy wasn't safely restored soon, Arum's position would be more precarious than ever.

'I think the washing can wait till I get back,' Mrs Mitchell was saying as she wiped down the sink. 'Goodness knows it won't take long to dry today, and every minute might count if that poor heifer's stuck somewhere.' Watching her, Lesley got the impression that her mother, like Val, despite all the worries, was actually enjoying having an emergency as an excuse to postpone everyday jobs and take part in some real action. In fact, neat and cool in shorts and a blouse, and hardly any bigger than Val, she could quite easily be another sister, and not a mother at all.

David brought Tassel along and accompanied them all to look at the tracks, but said he would have to return straight afterwards to rake the hay in the Ten Acre Paddock in preparation for baling.

'Dad will be using the tractor with the press, of course,' he said as they passed under the willowy archway into the River Paddock, 'but he reckons the land-rover will pull the rake all right, and we've really got to get moving to beat Smiler's thunderstorm.'

The sound of shouting and splashing reached them from the swimming-hole farther up-river, and Ian said enviously, 'Listen! Kids swimming. I wish it was me instead of them. Fancy having to spend a morning like this —'

An anguished wail from Val interrupted him. 'The tracks! Some lunatic's trampled all over them!'

'Those children swimming,' guessed Mrs Mitchell as they all crowded round to see the scuffled marks of thongs, sandals and bare toes where Val had found the heifer tracks earlier.

'They couldn't be expected to know, I suppose, but where do we go from here?'

'*I'm* going to bawl them out!' announced Val determinedly, heading for the river. Her mother hurried after her, intent on preventing ructions and bloodshed, but David followed too, and pointed out that it wouldn't be a bad idea to go down; one of them might have seen Gipsy.

The swimmers were town children, three boys and two girls known by sight to the Mitchells as the middle portion of Smiler Hodget's family. In complete contrast to their morose father, they were so boisterously cheerful as to annoy the now seriously worried Mitchells. No, they said carelessly, they hadn't seen a small brown heifer go off on her own anywhere.

Mrs Mitchell and David dragged away a seething Val, and Lesley and Ian followed till they were all out of earshot.

'So she could be anywhere,' David summed up, 'but I think your best bet is along the river. There are plenty of places where she could have got stuck in the logs and willows and the other flood junk, and there are patches of sand here and there. You might find some tracks farther upriver.' He hesitated, looking longingly at the willow-shaded river. 'I think you've copped the best job, really. Don't get too far away to come back and get the dinner, Mum! And good luck!' he called over his shoulder as he turned back to the hay-raking.

'Right!' said Mrs Mitchell, sounding so like Val in an organising mood that Val herself was startled. 'You girls go down-river and have a good poke around the uncleared bits, and Ian and I will take Tassel and go up-river and do the same. Don't make too much noise. If she's stuck somewhere she may call out. But call yourselves, she may answer. If none of us have any luck, we'll go up past the boundary fence.'

It was a long, arduous day for the Mitchells. When they assembled, sweaty and dispirited, for a late dinner, no one had seen any sign of the missing heifer, and even Val's optimism had waned. After a quick spell, Mr Mitchell returned to the tractor and Mrs Mitchell wearily began her housework, while David, Val, Lesley and Ian tackled what seemed to be the last resort for Gipsy, the Mines Department country south of the boundary fence, invariably referred to as the Bush. Beginning at the river, they trudged over it all afternoon, with wary eyes open for snakes as well as hoofprints.

At first the ground was easily covered, being flat and partly cleared between the river and the disused shale mines. Farther back, it gradually became sloping, then rocky, and finally thickly wooded and almost precipitous on the steeply rising shoulder of Shale Hill.

A little away from the mines, on the river side, stood the main parental justification of the rule that no young Mitchell was allowed into the bush unaccompanied. This was the caretaker's shack, an unprepossessing but harmless looking building of unpainted weatherboard. The objection, of course, was not to the shack itself, but to its occupant, a big, silent individual who was usually in a state of complete inebriation.

'Drunk as usual, I expect,' said David, disgustedly noting the untidy accumulation of bottles behind the shack as the four of them assembled round it. 'Reckon we should ask him about Gipsy?'

'If she came up and knocked at his door he probably wouldn't notice,' Val said scathingly, collapsing on to a log in the shade while they discussed it. Ian examined the dusty track to the door and said she hadn't – there were no hoof-prints.

'I suppose he can't hurt us if we just ask him,' Lesley said dubiously. 'There are four of us, and we should follow up every possibility.'

'O.K.,' said David, and pounded on the door, which threatened to fall in under his onslaught. Noticing this, Val said in an undertone, 'This is one of those places you hear about that's only kept together by the termites holding hands!'

After a few minutes' silence, David and Val and Lesley went round to try the back door, making impolite remarks to each other about the general state of squalor, but Ian insisted on remaining where he was in case the Caretaker tried to escape out the front way. It soon became apparent that he wasn't at home, however. 'Unless he's dead drunk under the bed,' said Val disrespectfully, peering through the dirty window. They collected Ian and picked their way through the litter of broken bottles towards the shale mines.

'I suppose he could be fishing,' said David, 'or getting provisions, or something.'

'Probably away stocking up on grog,' said irrepressible Val.

'Why do they keep him there?' Lesley wondered aloud.

'There isn't anything to caretake any more, and I can't see him being much use, anyhow.'

'I think he caretakes our wood for Dad,' said David, eyeing appreciatively the good-sized heap of wood cut from the bush and left to dry a few months earlier by his father and himself. 'Not actively, of course, but I s'pose his presence sort of deters any would-be wood thieves.'

'Wouldn't deter me,' muttered Val, skirting the stack without a glance and heading straight for the strange, leaning chunks of concrete which Lesley thought looked like huge, drunken tombstones dancing, but were actually relics of shale works.

Behind these were the dark, eerie mine-openings themselves, strictly forbidden, but who would want to venture into their damp, dangerous depths anyway? Much farther back, high on the steep sides of the hill, were the most dangerous holes of all: the vertical ventilation shafts, reputed to be eighty feet deep.

'But there are all sorts of other weird holes lower down around here,' David was saying. 'It's a pity, really. This flat part's got good soil and it's not used any more. It would make good grazing, if it weren't for the worry of your cattle falling down holes.'

Lesley shuddered. 'I suppose that makes it a likely place to find Gipsy,' she said apprehensively.

'Well, it would be, but there aren't any indications of her being here, and you must know after last night how many signs a straying heifer leaves!'

'At any other time the exploration of the Shale Works area would have been thoroughly enjoyed by the young Mitchells, but in the circumstances, they were just too hot and tired and worried. All were wearing lightweight tops and hats against the blistering sun, but the bush and the blackberries made heavy jeans necessary, and their mother had insisted on sturdy, snakeproof shoes that were almost unbearable in the sticky, oppressive heat. Their weariness was brought about by an exhausting, unsuccessful day of searching after a broken night. Their worries, heavy even on Ian's shoulders, seemed too numerous to bear, and appeared to increase as the day wore on.

That Friday evening there was no jumping in the Clover Paddock, although Mr Mitchell had baled all the hay there and was beginning on the Ten Acre. The sultry humidity was still almost unbearable, but the sky had become overcast, and threatening dark clouds were banking over Shale Hill. When the two hay carters arrived at about six o'clock, Smiler said he reckoned they had less than half an hour before the storm broke, and went to help David unhitch the hay rake from the land-rover.

Bruce dumped his bicycle, took off his jacket, and said sympathetically to Lesley, 'They tell me one of your heifers turned up missing. Found her yet?'

'No, and we've been looking all day. But how did you know?'

'Smiler said his kids told him you were out looking for her this morning. Any idea what's happened to her?'

Lesley shook her head and sighed, pushing her hair away from her clammy forehead. 'Arum opened a gate with her nose and let six of them out last night. We thought we'd got them all back, but this morning there were only five. And the awful thing is, she's a stud heifer, an awfully expensive one we'd just bought.'

Bruce nodded commiseratingly, then said suddenly, 'Where was she bought from, do you know?'

'Dad got her from Valleywood, less than a week ago,' she said drearily. 'Why?'

'Only about ten miles, and just a few days ago! Has

anyone rung up the Valleywood place to see if she's headed back?'

Lesley looked up quickly. 'That's a good idea. I don't think anyone thought of it. I mean, it's not as if she's a dog or anything. Do you think a heifer would?'

'You'd know more about that than I would,' said Bruce candidly. 'It was just a layman's stab in the dark.'

'Dad's over in the Ten Acre,' said Lesley, frowning, 'but I could dash in and get Mum to ring up Mr McGuire. Oh, blow!' she added as the land-rover roared out of the implement shed, free of the hay rake at last. 'I s'pose they'll want me to drive now, to keep more men for the bales.'

'Is Val around?'

'No, she's bark painting. There's Ian, though, on the land-rover. I'll send him.'

Ian took her message and departed, grumbling that it was not fair. He was forced to tramp around in the heat after lost heifers, but not even allowed to drive the land-rover in the paddock. Lesley would gladly have swapped places with him, in order to hear what Mr McGuire had to say, instead of carrying on the now familiar and dull routine of clutch, accelerator: pause, crawl forward, when she was flopping with fatigue.

'You look pretty knocked up,' said David, walking alongside the driver's window as she headed for the next bale. 'Don't fall asleep at the wheel, will you?' He strode ahead to pick up the bale. Bruce came up while the land-rover was stopped and said, 'Lesley, when you go in, will you tell your sister not to bother about Mum's bark paintings? If she's as exhausted as you, she'll be cursing my order!'

'No, she won't,' said Lesley seriously, dejectedly remembering the Pony Project. 'She needs the money for a very urgent cause.'

'Ah, of course! Christmas shopping!'

Christmas! Lesley thought with a shock, letting in the clutch. Just over a week away, but she hadn't thought of it for days. How un-Christmassy it would be if Gipsy were not found safe, if Arum had to be sold, or if, as had happened two years ago, vagaries of the weather made it necessary to spend all Christmas day labouring frantically in the hay paddocks to save the harvest. She sighed heavily at the thought. Then, right on cue, it began to rain. First a clap of thunder with dismal preliminary drizzle, which gathered force until great drops were pelting down. The rain clouds gathered across the sky like heavy eyebrows drawn together in a frown and, except for the occasional lightning flash, everything darkened so swiftly that Lesley had to switch on the headlights as well as the windscreen-wipers. In their probing gleam she saw Ian running towards the land-rover; breathlessly he piled into the cab at the next stop.

'I think Smiler's storm's begun!'

'Really? I hadn't noticed,' said Lesley sarcastically; but she was too urgently curious to maintain this attitude, and demanded: 'Well, did Mum ring up Mr McGuire?'

'She thought it was worth trying, but Mr McGuire said he hadn't seen anything of Gipsy. Then he said what about putting a Lost Ad in tomorrow's paper, so Mum sent me out to ask Dad how much he could afford for a reward. And she's rung the police, too.'

'How much —' began Lesley, but stopped as her father, wet and harassed-looking, opened the driver's door.

'Shove over, Les. Got to get this lot into the barn.'

Lesley shoved over on top of Ian, and Mr Mitchell changed into second.

'The load's not full yet, is it?' said Ian, indignantly elbowing Lesley in the ribs.

'No, but at least what we've got on is still dry. The men are stooking the rest so it won't get quite so wet. If it hadn't been for this damn storm we'd have got the whole lot in tonight.'

He nosed the land-rover into the shelter of the half-filled barn, yanked on the hand-brake and got out, calling over his shoulder as he hurried back to the hay paddock, 'You kids get yourselves inside quickly. There's nothing else you can do.'

Ian and Lesley pulled faces at each other, both intent on disobeying, and followed their father. But by the time they reached the Home Paddock gate, their shirts and shorts were saturated. Through the rain and the grey half-light they could see hunched figures bending and heaving bales into pyramids of three. They paused there for a moment, with the rain growing colder against their backs. Ian's determination was waning fast; Lesley yawned as she dismally compared this grim urgency with the cheerful fun of yesterday evening, before all the trouble had started. A roll of thunder decided her, and she turned round.

'Come on, Ian. We'll have to go back, or Dad will be mad. Anyway I've just remembered. I've got to check up on Arum before I go to bed.'

9 Telephone call

The young Mitchells would have found it terribly difficult to get out of bed on Saturday morning without the hope that Gipsy might have returned to spur them on. But a pre-milking inspection by David and Mr Mitchell showed nothing, and a pre-calf feeding look around by Val and Lesley proved that the wayward heifer had not found her way home during the night. Ian didn't even bother to look, but raced out early to the mail-box and tore back with a handful of Christmas cards and the *Advocate* opened at the *Lost and Found* column.

' "Lost: yearling Jersey heifer, ear tattoo: JMG 847. $10 reward," and our phone number.'

'Ten dollars reward,' said Lesley wonderingly.

'Yes, she's a valuable heifer, and your father thought that would encourage children on holiday to look for her,' said Mrs Mitchell, slicing bread at the table. She glanced at the kitchen clock, then out of the window. 'Nearly nine. Surely Jim and David haven't gone out to the hay paddocks before breakfast?'

'They got nearly all the Clover Paddock in last night,' said Ian, 'but the rest of it had to be stooked, and so did the baled part of the Ten Acre. P'raps some of the stooks have fallen over, like they did last year.'

Mrs Mitchell glanced up as the kitchen door opened, but it was only Val, carrying the two bark paintings she had brought to show her mother.

'They're the ones I finished last night, that Bruce wants

for his mother,' she explained, setting them on the window sill.

Ian said he couldn't wait a minute longer for breakfast, and began shovelling in cornflakes, but Lesley and Mrs Mitchell both got up to admire the paintings.

To look at them with the morning sunlight catching the glass of their frames was almost like looking into a viewer to see a colour slide. One showed a swampy paddock with leaning wooden fences and clumps of ti-trees and rushes; the other depicted a country road characteristically curving round a huge gum-tree like Guara's own. Both were typically Tasmanian scenes in muted greys and greens with an earthy red colour for the road, and shining white strips for the stretches of water in the swamp. Both were very different in context to the red, orange and black creations in the *Women's Weekly*, but in every other way they were easily comparable, and Lesley was newly amazed at Val's unexpected but undoubted talent with this marvellous, inexpensive material.

'You're improving all the time, darling,' Mrs Mitchell commented delightedly. 'These are really beautiful, I'll hate to see them go. How much are you going to charge for them?'

'Well, they're six inches by eight, and the frames were a dollar twenty each, and I spent about three hours on each one. What do you think, Mum?'

Before Mrs Mitchell could reply, the door opened again, and this time it was her husband and son, both wearing expressions of depression and worry that would have done credit to Smiler Hodgets himself. David swooped on the paper to see the advertisement, and Mr Mitchell washed his hands at the sink amid demands to know what was wrong. Then he slumped into his chair, wearily wiped his forehead, and began slowly slicing a banana on to his cornflakes, so dejectedly that everyone glanced to David for explanation.

'It's just one thing after another,' David said despondently, laying down the paper. 'First the heifer, the most promising animal on the place, then that rainstorm in the middle of pressing and carting in, and now a crook cow. Sharon. Isn't it unbelievable the way things happen to your top animals? Our highest producing cow last year. Last night she wouldn't eat, this morning she only gave about six pints of milk. She's only been in a week, but she started off with four gallons a day!'

'Is it milk fever?' asked Ian interestedly.

David rolled his eyes in exasperation. 'My dear, dumb, demented brother, milk fever is caused by making too *much* milk and characterized by paralysis of the hindquarters. And it occurs at *calving time*,' he added with finality, starting his breakfast.

Ian subsided, squashed, but Mrs Mitchell said worriedly, 'Do you know what is wrong with her, Jim?'

Her husband shook his head sighed heavily. 'She seems to have fallen away to nothing overnight. I ought to get the vet, but Barnett charges twice as much to come out on weekends. I'll have a look in my vet book, and if she doesn't get any worse we'll hold out till Monday.' He vented his opinion of the local vet in a few well-chosen words he normally didn't use in front of his children, but the family knew it was just an outlet for his general feelings of exasperation. Andrew Barnett, though unconventional, was a respected man highly skilled at his job. Slightly roused by his own descriptive ability, Mr Mitchell then began applying it to last night's weather, and demanded the newspaper so that he could see the forecast. 'Cloudy and cool, with isolated thunderstorms' on page one gave him further opportunities for more well-chosen remarks on the hard lot of the dairy farmer. Farther on through the paper he looked up and asked, 'When was that fire at Valleywood?'

'Last Friday night,' said David, 'we heard about it and got the heifers on Saturday morning. Why?'

'Just wondered. There's another poor devil on a dairy farm got nearly burnt out at Devonport yesterday.'

'Only a week between them!'

'Yes. Bit early in the season for that kind of thing. Oh . . . it says farther down it was an electrical fault. Apparently the storm last night came along just in time to put it out.'

'An ill wind —' began Val ironically, but her father had turned to the weather pattern on the last page and was complaining about the badly arranged highs and lows and fronts on the map. His family made sympathetic noises, though the early sun was still shining briskly and the humidity had dropped.

'Which is just as well,' said Val later over the washing-up, 'as we'll probably be out all day looking for that unspeakable heifer. I'm going out looking on Arum today, anyhow. It's all her fault, but all she does is doze under the willow-tree, waking at intervals for sustenance, while I slog all over the countryside, half-cooked and eaten alive, trying to right her wrongs. And the rest of my time I spend sitting on my backside gluing my fingers together in order to save her useless carcass by buying another useless horse that'll probably be just as much trouble. I'm beginning to think Silly Lily isn't worth it!'

'It's not Arum we're trying to save,' disagreed Lesley, wielding the tea-towel. 'It's ourselves, from having to slog around the countryside on foot the way you said, instead of on horseback. If Arum was sold, she'd probably be just as happy, perhaps happier if she had horsey company and a nice owner.'

'Nonsense,' said Val. 'Nice people don't buy horses like our Harum Scarum Mare-um, and other horses wouldn't even recognize her as equine. Dogs' meat is what she'd be, so we'd better find that heifer and make lots of bark paintings, quick-smart.'

Lesley knew that this prediction was an exaggeration, that was just Val's way to talk like this, and that she would really be very upset if Arum were sold, though she probably wouldn't show it. Nevertheless it made her uneasy, but the subject was automatically dropped when Mrs Mitchell brought some more dirty plates to be washed. Lesley went back to the table to clear away the milk jug and salt and pepper. The conversation here, over second cups of tea, was even less cheering, because it was more serious. It was about Gipsy, of course.

'At least I can come out too, today, while the hay dries out,' Mr Mitchell was saying. 'We'll just have to go over the farm with a fine-toothed comb and hope that other people will be looking out for her outside. But if we don't find her today, she's almost certainly dead of something, somewhere.'

'Dead of what?' Lesley cried, horrified at this pessimistic attitude.

Her father looked round at her, concerned. He hadn't realised she was there. 'Snake-bite, perhaps, dear, or possibly even drowning. And you know what could happen if she got into the bush and fell down one of those mine-shafts – though most of them are blocked up now. I don't see how she could still be walking round without somebody seeing her.'

'Perhaps someone will, after this ad,' said David,

reluctantly getting up. 'It's amazing how observant ten dollars will make some people. And with us doing the whole farm all day, she has to be found.'

'The trouble is,' observed Ian, 'it's much worse than looking for a shoe or something you've lost, because a cow moves around (if she's all right) and you've got to keep looking in the same places. It's not like just searching one place at a time and ticking it off.'

Arrangements were made and instructions given for systematic searching. Val went to get Arum and Mr Mitchell left with David and Ian, whom he was driving as far as the bush boundary in the land-rover. Lesley paused in the kitchen to pour out a bowl of milk for the cats, who were both asking politely, and was presently joined by her mother, who had been shaking the tablecloth outside.

'Has Val gone, dear?'

'Yes, out to get Arum. Did you want her, Mum?'

Mrs Mitchell folded the tablecloth thoughtfully. 'I just wanted to talk to her about Arum for a minute to make doubly sure she doesn't start opening gates again.'

'We're being extra careful,' said Lesley, putting the milk back in the fridge. 'We straightened up her fence again and made all the gates pony-proof. And we check up on her last thing every night. Mum . . . is Daddy really going to have to sell her?'

'No, darling, not if she doesn't cause any more trouble. I know what it's like to have a pony. I had my Jess from when I was about your age until I got married. And it doesn't cost a thing to keep Arum as long as she only needs that little paddock. There's plenty of feed and plenty of hay; in fact, Dad was hoping to sell some this year. I think that's what's got him down – the storm last night, and Sharon, of course. And Gipsy. Ready, Les? We'd better get going.'

As they went out, the telephone rang in the hall, and Mrs Mitchell turned back to answer it while Lesley waited hopefully. If it was someone who had found Gipsy they would be saved another long day's searching and worry. Even if Dad did have to fork out ten dollars, surely he would think it worthwhile, to have his heifer back? Then, perhaps, Arum's crime would be forgotten, and if she, Lesley, could get a holiday job and add the proceeds to Val's bark painting money . . .

She heard running footsteps and her mother's voice saying, 'Lesley, run out and stop Dad. It's the police on the phone. A man has reporting hitting a Jersey heifer, just over the river from here.'

10 Continual seesaw

'I was just coming round the railway bend on the River Road,' Geoffrey Dixon was saying, in the cramped little office in front of the police sergeant's house. 'Only doing about thirty-five, towing the trailer. Next thing I knew, this heifer just appeared at the bottom of the bend, walking out into the road, and I swerved and braked simultaneously. It must have been the loose gravel on the side of the road, I think, but I'm a bit hazy about what happened then. Next thing I knew, I was sideways in the ditch with my trailer overturned and empty.'

'But you don't think the heifer was badly hurt?' Mr Mitchell probed anxiously.

'Hard to say, mate, but if I did touch her it was only a graze. She disappeared pretty smartly, and there was no blood about. But my bull, now . . .'

'You said it looked like a whole-coloured yearling Jersey heifer,' persisted Mr Mitchell. 'How can you be sure, if you hardly saw her?'

'I know a pure-bred and I know a yearling,' said Mr Dixon affrontedly. 'I'm a Jersey breeder myself. That's what I'm trying to say – I'd just been to collect a pedigreed youngster for my next herd sire. But I didn't have him tied, see, so when the trailer turned over, he disappeared too.'

'Holy mackerel!' said Jim Mitchell as light suddenly dawned. 'They're off together, somewhere on the other side of the river. I'd better go and reorganize my search party.' He scraped his chair back.

The police sergeant, who was new to the district and nervous, suddenly realised that the two men he was interviewing had rather taken over the situation, and he hastened to reassert himself.

'Just a minute, Mr Dixon. About your car and trailer . . .'

'I'll take him looking for his bull in my land-rover,' said Jim Mitchell easily, 'then drive him out to his car when it's upright again.'

'But Mr Mitchell,' the sergeant insisted anxiously, feeling that things were really getting out of hand. 'There's my report . . .'

'I'm sure we can fix that up later, Sergeant. The thing now is to track down our stock while they're still in the district. I'm a busy man at this time of the year, and I'm sure Mr Dixon is too.' He was at the door now, his hand on the knob.

'I'm afraid this is pretty irregular,' the sergeant began doubtfully, wiping his forehead, but now Mr Dixon had got up too.

'Right you are, mate. This is no time for a cockatoo conference. Thanks very much, Sarge, you've been a real help.'

The police station door was politely closed, and the harassed sergeant was left shuffling his papers in an ineffectual manner and helplessly watching their departure through an open window.

'Over the river!' exclaimed David in the tone of one who wants to kick himself. 'Why didn't we think of that? It'd only be up to her knees in most parts. There's that ford place just up from the swimming-hole where you can walk over in gumboots in summer.'

He and Lesley and Val and their mother were rattling

over the River Road in the Mitchells' elderly station-wagon in pursuit of Jim Mitchell and Geoff Dixon in the land-rover. Everyone was optimistic now, and they had all turned out in the hope of having Gipsy safely behind a wired-up gate before dinner time. The only exception was Ian, who said he reckoned the heifer was as good as found, now, and they wouldn't need him to help fetch her home, so he might as well go fishing.

The site of the car accident was not exactly opposite Guara, being several hundred yards up-river from the Mitchells' boundary fence. The river was quite close to the road on one side; on the other, sparse heath and bracken gave way to a fairly thin sprinkling of tall, skinny gums and the occasional blackwood or wild cherry.

Unfortunately, the only place where the searchers could expect to find tracks to begin on was covered with hard white gravel, so the plan was to spread out and move into the scrub, watching out for tracks on the softer ground, snakes, landmarks, colourful bark (a plea from Val) and, of course, the missing animals.

It was Mrs Mitchell who first caught sight of the movement that proved to be Geoff Dixon's yearling bull pulling at the wild snake-lilies in the shade of a blackwood tree. Everyone helped Mr Dixon corner him, and one of the two halters brought in readiness was in place after only a reasonable amount of anxious manoeuvring, gentle words in soothing tones, and one or two dubious moments. Once caught and haltered, the young bull became very docile, and the Mitchells sincerely admired his striking looks and the deep golden coat that shone like burnished copper when he was led out into the sun. But when further examination of the area failed to reveal Gipsy, disappointment fell again. Mr Dixon, delighted over the safe appearance of his bull, obligingly tied him to a tree and helped search till noon, when he had to sit through a long argument with the police sergeant before reclaiming his righted car and trailer and leaving for his farm. Then, after a quick, cold dinner, the Mitchells returned to the vicinity to carry on, having checked once again that Mr Dixon's description tallied with that of Gipsy.

'It must have been her,' said Mr Mitchell. 'There aren't any Jersey herds at all on this side of the river. And since it must have been her, she must be here somewhere!'

'Life's just one continual seesaw,' sighed Lesley. 'We keep thinking everything's all right, and then we're thwarted again. And I was sure she'd be here, practically waiting on the side of the road.'

'Oh, well,' said Val, whose pockets were bulging with bark. 'We're obviously down, now, so according to your seesaw programme, the next thing's up!'

It was after four o'clock that afternoon when they gave up; the one cheerful thing amid all the dreariness was that the sky was still as innocently blue as if it had never heard of rainstorms and the sun, merciless to weary searchers, was also flooding down on to the stooked bales of the Clover and Ten Acre Paddocks.

'It will be drying out the other paddocks, too,' said Mr Mitchell to David, who was riding with him in the land-rover. 'They should be ready for pressing on Monday.' He sighed as he turned the land-rover towards the dairy and looked over at the hay in the Ten Acre, which would have been in the barn but for the rainstorm. 'Hullo! Don't tell me that mad caretaker has lit a fire on a day like this!'

David looked across the hay paddocks and saw it too: a little ripple of smoke against the darker green-grey background of trees.

'Surely not,' he said doubtfully. 'I can't see him baking Christmas cake over a fire! We went to ask him about Gipsy yesterday, Dad, but there was no sign of him anywhere about. Just the usual collection of broken bottles . . . that sun! On the bottles! You don't think . . .?'

Mr Mitchell got up to stand on the land-rover step, shading his eyes. 'Flame! Suffering cats! I think the shack's on fire! And that lunatic caretaker is probably lying drunk somewhere.' He dived back into the land-rover and reversed, shouting to David, who had just got out, 'Get some empty bags out of the feed shed and dunk them in the trough!'

The station-wagon was just rounding the Maternity Ward, and he turned and beckoned to his wife to turn left instead of right. She pulled up in a cloud of dust outside the dairy.

'What's up, Jim?'

But Val, who had piled out with the others, had already noticed. 'There's a fire up near the shack!'

'Golly, the Caretaker!' Lesley exclaimed anxiously.

'Golly, our wood, you mean,' corrected David, tearing out of the dairy with an armful of dripping grain sacks. He dumped them on the back of the land-rover beside Ian, who had scrambled up, eager for excitement. Val made to climb up after him, and Lesley followed, but Mr Mitchell, who had been giving his wife instructions, turned and roughly ordered them down.

'Milking's late already. You kids help your mother. I'll send David back for the fire brigade if it's too big for us.'

He was clearly in no mood to hear arguments, so they hastily obeyed and the land-rover departed, roaring round the Ten Acre in top gear.

'Phew!' Val pushed back her pigtails, which had almost escaped from their rubber bands altogether during the long day. 'Fancy leaving us all here with hay on one side of that fire and bush on the other.'

'It doesn't look too bad, though.' Mrs Mitchell strained her shaded eyes. 'No wind at all, and things should still be pretty damp after that rain. What beats me is how it was dry enough for a fire to start in the first place. And the only thing that really *worries* me is the wood-heap.'

'It looks more to this side of the wood-heap,' Lesley said hopefully.

'The only thing that really worries *me*,' said Val, 'is all these calves and cows we have to deal with before we can collapse. Time for a drink first, Mum?'

'Several drinks,' Lesley added loudly, against Ian's continued grumbles about being left out of the excitement.

'Water from the dairy tap,' their mother said firmly. 'If we go back to the house we'll never get going.'

The cows had filed down the lane at their normal time, half an hour before, and were now standing placidly in the yard chewing the cud. Despite this, Ian unchained Tassel for a run while Lesley assembled the calf buckets and Val and her mother got on with the milking. Neither of them was very practised in the dairy, and with their constant trips to the door to peer through the shimmering heat at the progress of the fire, their own progress was somewhat erratic. Sharon was the very last cow in, and Mrs Mitchell was horrified at her condition.

'No wonder Jim was worried!' she exclaimed in consternation, noting the dull eyes and shrunken sides and feeling the slack udder. 'She's hardly worth milking, but try her with some bran, Val.'

Sharon disinterestedly nosed the proffered bran, and refused even to look at subsequent tempting offerings of new hay and cattle pellets, so they turned her out into the Maternity Ward, which was conveniently free of maternity cases that night. On the way back from shutting her in, Val's sharp eyes caught sight of the land-rover returning. Her resulting yell brought everyone out of the dairy, and the air was flying with urgent questions before the firefighters were even in earshot.

'Is it out?'

'What was burning?'

'Is the Caretaker all right?'

'What about the wood stack?'

The sacks on the tray were blackened and dry now, and the weary faces of Mr Mitchell and David were blackened, too – and anything but dry, the family saw as the land-rover pulled up. Mr Mitchell wiped his forehead and made it worse, and David began answering the questions.

'It was the shack, all right, but the fire started in the grass behind it, and I'm sure it was the sun on one of those bottles. Two of the walls were alight, and a bit of undergrowth, but we managed to put it out all right.'

'Where's the Caretaker?' interrupted Lesley.

'He's there,' her father said grimly. 'The silly old so-and-so hurt his leg stumbling around drunk, so he's even more useless than usual. His leg is all swollen up; I think he should be in hospital. Anyway' – getting out of the land-rover – 'I'm going to ring the ambulance now. And the police. We can't have a menace like that on our boundary, not in fire-danger periods. Goodness knows the Sergeant is a pretty useless type, but at least he's official. He can get in touch with the Mines Department.'

Mrs Mitchell went back to the house with him, but the four children stayed in the dairy to hose and sweep out the bales and yard, and wash the milking machine. At first, progress was very slow, as everyone wanted to listen to David's elaborations about the fire, but it soon speeded up. Lesley and Ian wanted to visit the scene, especially after the police sergeant's car was observed going up there. But David said he was dead beat, and for once Val was against more action and excitement.

'My only ambitions for the evening,' she said as they closed the dairy door, 'are tea and bed, in that order and in quick succession. And I hope Mum remembered to put about a gallon of cordial in the fridge so that I can hog the lot.'

'Arum's still in,' Lesley noted thankfully at the back gate.

'Yeah, but Gipsy's still out,' said David cynically.

'And Sharon's still sick,' added Val, 'And now this fire. I think our seesaw's broken down, Les. Three downs in a row, without a single up for variety. You'd better get underneath and start pushing.'

11 *Another lonely cow*

Valleywood Gipsy returned to drink at the shallow stretch of river she had crossed a few hours earlier. She gazed round alertly before lowering her muzzle to the water and sucking in great gulps. The weird, alarming cry of a native hen caught her attention for a moment, and she looked across the river to the other bank, which was greenly fringed with willows and their reflections. But she had no wish to go back over there. The strange compulsion to wander had vanished as suddenly as it had come. Now she was lonely, the herd instinct urging her to return, to find her mates, to be one of a number again. Her vague sense of direction had sent her back this way, but something was wrong; she had wandered up and down the river bank all afternoon, bewildered at finding no one. Now, refreshed, she was ready to try again. Neatly she shook shining water droplets from each dainty hoof, and scrambled across the coarse gravel to the dusty track beyond. The native hen called again, and she paused to look back. But the eddies she had made had widened and dwindled and levelled, the river had regained its evening tranquillity, and the native hen was silent. So the brown heifer set off across the partially cleared flats of the bush, heath and bracken rustling as her slender dark legs brushed past.

An unfamiliar smell beckoned, and she broke into a trot. It was not a cattle smell, it was rancid and a little frightening, but undoubtedly challenging. She followed it to the empty shell of the caretaker's shack, and spent some time sniffing around the charred wall and littered bottles with nervously dilated nostrils. The smell of man was still strong, but there as no life here now. Presently the heifer lost interest and followed the track to the right, where it wound up the rocky slope. She faltered uncertainly and look down on to the flat, then up at the forbidding bulk of Shale Hill. This was all wrong.

Suddenly, a faint familiar sound reached her through the quiet evening air, tugging at her instincts. She stiffened, legs braced, ears pricked, eyes bulging. There it was again, to the north. The unearthly bellow of another lonely cow. She lifted her head and answered eagerly, then turned and plunged straight down the slope into the ghostly shadows of the bush.

'I wish poor Sharon would stop bellowing,' was Lesley's last drowsy thought as she drifted into unconsciousness that night.

12 Hoofprints in the dust

On Sunday morning there was no question of anyone going to church. Although the Mitchells lived too far away to hear it, the church bell in the town rang before they had even knocked off for breakfast. Everyone had started work late and bleary-eyed, but so much was happening that they were soon wide-awake out of sheer necessity.

An almost constant hindrance to getting the work done was the succession of people, mostly schoolchildren, who kept turning up in the hope of acquiring the ten-dollar reward. The first had arrived the previous afternoon, but they continued to come on Sunday morning, either asking where the heifer had last been seen, or actually reporting finding her. Unfortunately, most of them had more enthusiasm than knowledge, and the Mitchells lost a great deal of time following up reports that turned out to be Hereford steers running loose, house cows from the town, or someone else's poddy calves.

'You wouldn't believe people could be so stupid,' Lesley was saying as she removed Fiona's empty milk bucket and led the little heifer out of the calf shed and into the top calf paddock. 'The only good thing that's come of it is that bark-painting order.'

Val grunted noncommittally, dumping calf pellets into a bucket.

'All very well for you to rejoice over orders. You don't have to make them. If I hadn't left those two on the window-sill, and Mum hadn't let those searchers into the kitchen to see Dad, they would never have thought of bark paintings for Christmas presents.'

'And we'd have missed out on about eight dollars for the Pony Project.' Lesley sighed. 'Talking about Christmas presents, it's a terrible time of the year to try to save up for anything. Even if I had any time to go Christmas shopping, I've hardly got any money to spend.'

'I'm going to give everyone bark paintings,' said Val more cheerfully. 'They take time to make, and it's an awful waste not to sell them, but they don't cost a thing without frames.'

'You are lucky to be able to make things like that so easily,' Lesley said enviously. 'I've tried and tried, but I just can't think of any way I could earn money, even if I didn't spend all day and every day looking for Gipsy and worrying about Arum.' She opened the gate for Val to take Supreme out. 'At least *he's* looking well. And isn't he growing fast!' She followed them out with the calf pellet bucket and emptied its contents into the calves' trough. 'This all they get?'

Val gave Supreme her fingers to suck, and led his muzzle down into the trough. 'It's plenty. These two are a bit young for them yet, but the earlier the better.' She eased a few pellets into the bull calf's milky mouth, and he tasted them reflectively before beginning to chew. 'Look! He's got the message already! He's not nearly as dopey as most big bulls.'

But after due deliberation, this big bull decided that the strange, hard little lumps were not for him. He had given them a fair trial, and now he spat them out and began hopefully sucking Fiona's ear. The girls laughed ruefully.

'I spoke too soon,' said Val, rescuing Fiona. 'Come on, Les, there are still nine big ones to do. And six more cows due this week. We'll be up to our eyeballs in calves soon.'

The calf-feeders finished before the milkers, but as Val and Lesley were scrubbing their milk buckets in the dairy wash-trough, their father hailed them from the cow bails. When they ran in, he shouted above the noise of the milking machine: 'Sharon hasn't come home, and David's busy. Will you two go down to the Creek Paddock to look for her?'

Val stared. 'We put her in the Maternity Ward last night. Didn't Mum tell you she was still looking seedy?'

Irritably Mr Mitchell removed the teat cups from a cow that had finished. 'Yes, but she didn't say you'd kept her home. I already knew the poor devil was seedy.' He sighed forgivingly. 'I reckon we were talking too much about the fire and everything. Sharon's not at the gate,' he added, looking over at the Maternity Ward. 'Must be in the shed.'

Suddenly apprehensive, Lesley ran after him as he strode across the yard to the calving shed. They both reached the door together and looked in. Sharon was standing in the corner, head down, eyes full, sides caved in, a personification of dejection. She stayed quite still and allowed Mr Mitchell to feel her udder without even turning to look at him.

'Slack as a bit of old rag,' he said heavily. 'And she hasn't eaten for days. You go and help David and Val finish in the dairy, Lesley. I'm going down to the house to ring the vet.'

Lesley nodded as he hurried out. Then she gently patted Sharon, who took no notice at all, before running back to the dairy.

'He's coming after he's been to church,' Mr Mitchell told them sardonically at breakfast time. 'I thought all vets were heathens without consciences, by the fees they charge, but apparently some of them profess to be Christians.'

He was in a scratchy mood, but nobody blamed him, although Val did venture to say that drugs, even for animals, were terribly expensive, and so was mileage to these country places. But she subsided obediently when her mother frowned warningly and steered the conversation off the shoals by saying, 'I wonder if the Mines Department will think it worthwhile repairing the Caretaker's shack?'

'The Sergeant told me last night that they wouldn't have the old Caretaker back,' replied Mr Mitchell, 'but I doubt if they'll find anyone else to live there, even with the burnt parts repaired. It's a pretty primitive old hovel.'

'What was the Sergeant doing up there after the ambulance left last night?' said David. 'I meant to ask at the time, but some kids with a poddy calf turned up and I got side-tracked.'

'Just poking round, I think. He's one of those annoying blighters who does everything by the book if it kills him. I suppose there's a list of essential things to be done at the scene of a fire and he does them, one after the other, in correct chronological order, and ticks them off as he goes!'

'*I* know!' exclaimed Ian through a mouthful of bread and honey. He swallowed about half of it and continued slightly more distinctly, 'You know that fire at Valleywood, before we got the heifers? They thought it was lit on purpose, didn't they? Then there was that other one at Devonport a couple of days ago. And now here! I bet the Sergeant's hot on the trail of some criminal with a thing about burning down dairy farms, and he was busy looking for clues!'

'Why dairy farms?' Lesley wondered. 'The last one was on Mines Department land.'

'And the second one was an electrical fault,' Mr Mitchell pointed out.

But Ian waived this and explained to Lesley, 'It was right on our boundary. It would have been here in no time if Dad hadn't seen it. And of course the criminal would have to make it look like someone else's fault. He probably sabotaged the electrical wiring at that other place.'

'But those broken bottles —' began David.

'Red herrings,' theorised Ian excitedly.

His father laughed and said, 'Even if that fantastic yarn could be true, I can't imagine our Sergeant is hot on anyone's trail.'

'Can't imagine him any better than lukewarm,' agreed Val, who had seen him last night.

But Ian was used to overcoming dampeners from his elders, and he put this one to good use by saying, 'Well, in that case, he probably missed all the clues, and we'd better go up and have a look round.' He looked hopefully at his sisters. 'Val, will you come and help?'

'Too much bark painting to do,' she said unconvincingly; it would have been fun to poke around the shack with its grim occupant out of the way.

'You'll come, Les?'

'I'm going out to look for Gipsy, on Arum, since Val won't be wanting her.'

'You can look for Gipsy as well as clues in the bush.'

'We looked there; have you forgotten?' enquired David; but his father said thoughtfully, 'I think it'd be a good idea for you kids to go up there and clear away those bottles. You shouldn't have to, but we don't want a repetition of last night, and the Mines Department might never do it. Goodness knows there are plenty of people looking for Gipsy now, and David and I are going to search over the river again after the vet's been.'

'Don't forget,' teased David, 'that if you find a bundle of oil-soaked rags in the bush, you mustn't touch it with your hands or you'll mess up the finger-prints. Better borrow a pair of Mum's gardening gloves!'

'And a magnifying glass,' added Val.

'And a suitcase to put the clues in,' Lesley contributed.

'And a camera for photographing the Scene of the Crime,' Val suggested, warming to the idea.

'Handcuffs,' said David, 'in case you make an arrest!'

'Arum can be the Black Maria!'

'Talking of Arum,' said Val, suddenly serious, 'we must take a halter to tie her up with. If you try to lead her round while you're doing anything, she walks on it.'

To Ian's relief, David abandoned the game too, as someone rode up the lane on a bicycle. 'Looks like Bruce, but he knows we're not carting-in till tomorrow.'

It was Bruce, but not for the carting-in. 'I was going to ring up and see if you'd found your heifer,' he said after greeting the Mitchells, 'but I thought I might as well come over and pick up my bark paintings, too.' He looked enquiringly at Val.

'Your paintings are those two on the window-sill, if they're O.K.,' she said, 'and we haven't found Gipsy.'

'Maybe you could use a willing addition to the search-party, then,' Bruce suggested to Mr Mitchell. 'I've got all day – golly, Val, you certainly can do it!' He sounded really pleased, a bark painting in each hand. 'Wouldn't like to give me lessons for a consideration, would you? You can get a lot of money for things like these in the right arty places!'

Val said offhandedly that lessons weren't necessary, just practice, and anyone could do it if they tried.

Lesley followed her mother's example and carried a

stack of plates to the sink. 'No, they can't. *I* can't. I don't seem to have any money-making talents.'

Mrs Mitchell overheard, and resolved to make sure her second daughter had something to spend for Christmas, but she had no chance to do anything about it then, as Ian, having cleaned up everything edible at the table, was urging his sisters on with the washing-up. 'Before the Sergeant gets here and finds all the clues.'

'What clues?' asked Bruce, and was immediately told by four people at once, with so many witty sallies that he never really did find out, and presently went outside to see Sharon with Mr Mitchell and David. They were soon followed by Lesley, who returned to the back gate with Arum and got involved in a heated argument that just because she caught the pony, it didn't necessarily follow that she rode it.

'It does follow! I went all the way to catch her and bridle her —'

'While I was washing up!' interjected Val.

'And I was going to ride her this morning anyway! You were going to do bark paintings —'

'To raise money to buy *your* horse,' Val reminded her unkindly.

'As if this one is yours! She was a family pony to begin with, so why should she be more yours than mine? I look after her just as much as you do!'

'I was looking after her before you could even reach to put her bridle on!'

'Just because you're older! Anyway, that means you've already had more riding than me, so it's *my turn*!'

No doubt Val would have thought up an answer even to this one if Ian hadn't interfered by stepping between them and yelling impatiently, 'Look, will you two shut up! The morning's half over already. We can't all ride Arum, so why not leave her home?'

'Because I fetched her and I'm riding her!' shouted Lesley, losing her temper, and she scrambled on to Arum's back before Val could stop her, and cantered away down the dairy track.

Frustrated, Val turned on Ian. 'You great lunatic! Now we both walk all the way, just to pick up bottles. And don't talk to me about clues! I've had enough of it!'

'I wasn't going to. I was just wondering why you girls are always bickering over that horse. Dave and I haven't got things about horses. *I* just wish I could drive the tractor.'

Val's anger always abated fast, and now she stuck her hands in her pockets and considered what Ian had said. 'I don't know. I reckon it's a general thing that girls like horses better than cars and motor-bikes. Most of them. And, of course, we're too young to drive, anyway. We can get around by walking, or biking, or – like that.' She gestured at the flying dot that was Arum and Lesley in the distance. 'Riding just turns some kids on the way motor-bikes do others. And it's such a challenge to train a horse, even a half-witted one.' She sighed. 'Sometimes I think one pony per family is worse than none at all.'

Lesley swung Arum through the gateway to the left and galloped her down the Ten Acre Paddock. She knew she was being silly, knew she would regret this later on, but however much she told herself so, she couldn't make herself believe it. She was in the right. Val was unreasonable, selfish and unfair, and it was her turn to walk. The argument drummed over in her mind, in time with Arum's hoofs drumming on the hard ground, and gradually, the more she thought about it, the more ridiculous it seemed to go tearing off in a huff like that.

It always took Lesley a while to cool down, but the excitement of galloping flat-out helped; so did the overwhelming, heady scent of the drying hay beneath Arum's flying hooves. That is, the *hay* is below, Lesley corrected herself. The actual fragrance rose around and above her, warm and hazy, the smell of sunshine spiced with the tang of the moisture it was drawing from the cut grass and clover. The result was a unique scent that flooded lavishly into her brain, reminding her of daydreams and honey bees and the way cats smelt when they had been mousing in a barn. It also prodded memories of other summers, evoking a wistful regret that summer faded so soon, and a whole year must pass before it would be there again. By the time Lesley reached the boundary fence, she was wondering whether she could somehow capture the scent and make her fortune as a perfume manufacturer. When Arum automatically bounced to a halt, she was jolted back to reality, and registered immediate shame as she recalled her trivial argument and reckless departure.

She looked back over the ten acres of neat windrows. Val and Ian were just rounding the dairy. They would reach her in about five minutes. If she just waited at the boundary for them, things might be awkward, but they could be even worse if she rode back and offered Arum and Val refused. The only thing seemed to be to go on, to be picking up bottles when they arrived and see what sort of mood Val was in then. With a bit of luck, Ian might have calmed her down. Lesley slid from Arum's back and had a short wrestling match with the gate, which was a difficult one in order to discourage town children from opening it on their way to the river, and possibly leaving it down. After several seconds' struggling, Lesley decided that there was a flaw in this reasoning;

the gate was openable, but she, for one, simply couldn't shut it. Therefore, other children would likely face the same problem, and simply do what she was going to have to do – leave it open. But at least she knew there was no possibility of any cattle straying through the hay paddock during the morning, and the combined efforts of the three of them on the way back would surely conquer the stiff wire.

She heaved herself on to Arum again, and picked a way for her down the stony, potholed track. It had once been a road for motor vehicles, but years of disuse had allowed blackberries to sprawl over it. Branches of the wattles and gums on either side brushed at Lesley's arms and hair, sometimes meeting in an archway over her head. As she descended, the trees thinned, the track levelled and widened, then faded away altogether as it reached the cleared ground behind the Caretaker's shack.

After David's description of the night before, Lesley had expected a charred wall and a patch of singed grass. The reality startled her so much that she wondered for a moment if there had been another fire later. But there couldn't have been, for who would have put it out? She found a shady place to tie Arum, absently patted her neck, and approached the shack. It was strange to be in the bush alone, even stranger not to be giving this part a wide berth, and quite shocking to see the extent of the damage. Acrid-smelling burnt grass crunched under her shoes and covered about an acre of ground behind her. She made her way past charred boxes and the heap of blackened bottles. And the shack! All of two walls and part of the roof was burnt jaggedly away, with some stronger splinters of wood hanging down like black stalactites from the beams. The other walls were badly singed, and the glass in their windows was smoke-coloured.

Lesley made her way round the side of the shack, her eyes on the ground to avoid stepping on broken bottles. She squeezed between a derelict dog-kennel and the blackened meat-safe, hanging from a nail with its door swinging. And stopped dead. There, on the ground just a few feet from the front of the shack, was a cowpat.

Lesley's mind whirled. 'Don't think it,' she told herself dizzily, running forward. But the pat was fresh, dropped recently in the midst of a criss-cross of dainty hoofprints in the dust, and she couldn't help thinking it. Feverishly she darted around, looking for a single line of tracks leading away from the empty shack. Out by the Mitchell's wood-heap she found it, leading right to the track that wound up to the shale works. Another dung-pat, and she was running up the hill. Please God! It must be Gipsy!

It can't be, reason told her sternly. *You looked here, didn't you, up this very track? And weren't David and Dad here last night?*

Yes! But they didn't notice! She must have been here afterwards. It can't be anything else!

If it was Gipsy, why is there only one set of tracks? reason persisted relentlessly. *She must be still on the hill. Somewhere up there.* Lesley paused to look up at Shale Hill in awe, just as Gipsy had done. *Think of the shale works, and all the holes and open mines.* Oh, no! She pushed down the thought and forced her aching legs on up the hill. Gipsy *must* be all right!

Suddenly she was in the middle of the shale works, surrounded by the huge concrete slabs she had once likened to drunken tombstones. Goodness knows what they were ever used for, she thought, looking wildly around. The tracks had petered out on the hard, black, shaley ground. Supports for the processing machinery, Dad had thought, but now all that remained of the machinery were odd bolts and bars cemented into the slabs, and twisted pieces of rusty iron scattered around. And the concrete slabs would no longer support anything much, keeling over like that. One great cube ahead was lying right over like an uprooted tree.

'Now I know what turmoil is,' Lesley thought, casting around desperately for tracks. Such was her agitation that when she rounded the overturned slab and saw the brown heifer trapped in the cavity the slab had left, she just stood there blinking giddily for a few seconds, unable to comprehend the message of her eyes to her brain. *It's her! There she is! You've found her!*

Then a movement of Gipsy's head stirred Lesley into action and she came slowly forward, the heifer's wide, frightened eyes following every move.

The hole was incredibly deep compared with the size of the concrete pillar whose jagged base was still lying half in it. Gipsy was trapped half under the concrete, lying awkwardly on her side with her hips wedged between it and another, smaller, broken piece of concrete that had fallen askew into the hole. The black shale was scored deeply with evidence of the heifer's struggles. She had blood on both hips and the only visible shoulder blade, and was now slumped from exhaustion.

Desperately, Lesley put her shoulder to the huge concrete chunk and shoved with all her strength, but, as she had expected, with no effect. She stood back despairingly, a hundred possible and impossible courses of action rushing through her head. The terrible bleeding gashes – rags to wash them and stop the flow? That panting tongue – water in a tin? The cruel, unyielding concrete – someone strong – several people – to move it. Perhaps Arum – Val – Ian? In a flurry of indecision she hesitated, then turned and raced down the hill.

13 The steeplechase bit

Val and Ian barely had time to register surprise at the deserted pony and empty hut before Lesley burst out of the scrub near the woodstack.

'I've found Gipsy! But she's hurt – stuck in a hole up at the shale works. Hurry *up*! We've got to get her out!'

'You've found her? How badly hurt?' demanded Val, diving towards the track.

Lesley pounded behind her, breathless from running and anxiety. 'I can't tell, but she's bleeding. Come *on*, Ian!'

Reluctantly Ian turned away from the fascinating burnt-out shack and followed more slowly up the hill.

'How on earth did you come to be up here?' gasped Val, now also breathless from exertion.

'There were – lots of tracks – round the front of the shack. Must have – been there last night. They – led up here – and I – followed. There – over by the – tombstone.'

They ran on to the flat shale works' platform.

'My sainted Aunt! The poor thing!'

Lesley could see Val competently sizing up the situation and was ashamed of her own dithering inadequacy in the same position.

'If we can find a very strong sapling, we *might* lever that lump off her . . . Where the heck's Ian?'

Ian arrived a few moments later to find his sisters rushing round the platform like ants. When they had selected what Val considered to be a suitable pole, he soon found himself on one end of it while she poked the other under the side of the concrete slab. But even the three of them together could move it only about half an inch, and Val called off operations for fear of hurting the heifer.

'It should be lifted off her slowly and steadily.' She frowned, leaning against another slab and rubbing her sore hands. 'What about those bolts stuck in the top?'

Lesley thought hard, absently leaning over to rub Gipsy sympathetically behind the ears. But she must have moved her hand too quickly, for the heifer rolled her eyes and panicked. After a night's struggling, this final terrified jerk, perhaps coupled with the half-inch movement of the slab, freed her hips from the wedge, and she slipped deeper into the hole.

Lesley gazed at her in horror, but Val was there in a second.

'Good grief! We'll never get her out if she goes any farther!' Gingerly she lowered herself down beside Gipsy, bracing her back against the helpless shoulder to make the heifer more comfortable. 'Ian, you get down there and support her hips. Cripes, they've bled a lot! Everyone's hankies, please.'

Ian eased himself into position and passed a grubby handkerchief. 'She's not struggling now, is she? You reckon she's broken something?'

'Heavens, I *am* a dolt! No, Les, don't come down. Get Arum and race home. The vet's probably still there. Gipsy's sure to need him if we ever get her out, and it'll save calling him twice, if you get there before he leaves. We'll stay here and support her. Tell Dad the position. He'll probably want the tractor and hoist to get her out, and the trailer to take her home. Hurry up!'

But Lesley was already pounding on the shale track for the third time that morning. Arum leaned back on her halter rope in astonishment at the flying figure rushing out of the scrub, but that was nothing to her astonishment at having her bridle snatched off the fence, the bit bundled into her mouth, the head-piece crammed over her outsized ears, and the throat-lash left flapping wildly under her chin; all without a word or a pat or any proper consideration. Lesley yanked the halter rope undone from the fence, added the end to her tangled handful of reins, and vaulted on to the bony shoulder. With two reins and a rope in one hand and a good tuft of mane in the other, she dug her heels into Arum's ribs and they were gone, leaving only a flurry of ashes behind.

'This is Brian Robinson,' said Andrew Barnett, introducing him to Mr and Mrs Mitchell, David and Bruce. 'He's taking over when I leave for England in January.'

The new vet shook hands shyly. He was about thirty years old, short and fair and a little nervous-looking, in complete contrast to the assurance of his older colleague. 'Looks more like a dog and cat man,' Mrs Mitchell thought. David tried to imagine him coping with a bull in pain or a colicky horse, and couldn't. Mrs Mitchell saw that the menfolk were warily sizing each other up, and firmly led the way to the sick pen, saying she knew they didn't want to be held up, and the sick cow was just in here.

'Acetonaemia,' said Mr Barnett ten minutes later, expertly plugging a needle into Sharon's jugular vein. 'Reduced level of glucose – just as milk fever is caused by loss of calcium. Another thing in common with milk fever: it usually hits high producers. You can drench them with molasses in the early stages, or glycerine, but in these circumstances, a jab in the jugular is best.'

'It came on so suddenly I hardly noticed any early stages,' Mr Mitchell said apologetically.

The vet deftly removed his needle and told David he could take off the halter now.

'Suspect it as soon as a cow starts falling away in condition. You can test for it yourself. I'll give you some tablets. White. You test the cow's urine with them. If they turn blue, it's acetonaemia.'

While David and Bruce let Sharon out, Mr Barnett washed his hands in the dairy, then went out and opened the boot of his car. It was crammed with boxes and bottles and jars, ropes and chains, clean pairs of overalls and fearsome objects like trocars and an electric goad. To everyone else it looked like a hopeless jumble, but the vet knew just where to find what he needed. He thrust his hand into the motley collection and produced a small bottle which he gave to Mr Mitchell.

'For diagnosing your next case. If you get a positive reaction, ring me up – no, we're leaving for England in a month. Ring Brian at the surgery and he'll send you out a drench.'

Brian Robinson nodded shyly. He hadn't spoken a word throughout the visit. 'But of course he's hardly had a chance to,' Mrs Mitchell thought charitably, 'the way the other bloke natters on.'

Andrew Barnett was getting out of his overall, admiring the good condition of the other Guara animals as he did so. 'Nice to see a decently reared mob of calves. Your herd's a credit to you, Jim.'

The Mitchells in turn said politely that it was nice for him to be going to England. Mr Mitchell thanked the vet for the tablets, and despite his impatience to be out looking for his heifer, apologized again for calling him out on Sunday. Finally, to everyone's relief, Messrs Barnett and Robinson climbed into the car and took their leave. Ten seconds after the vet's shiny new Rover turned cautiously down the potholed road, it was followed by the Mitchell's ancient land-rover, with Mr Mitchell, David and Bruce on their way to the other side of the river. A mere five seconds after this, Lesley pelted into the yard on Arum to find only her mother walking leisurely back to the house.

Reining in the excitedly prancing pony, Lesley yelled, 'Mum, has the vet gone?'

'Just this minute,' said Mrs Mitchell, indicating the departing car.

Lesley followed her pointing finger and saw the land-rover as well, to her horror. 'Help! Dad's gone too!' She lifted her heels, but Arum needed no urging. Her blood was up, and she was away before the heels contacted her sides.

'LESLEY! What's the matter?'

Lesley turned her head to answer; her loose hair flew round her face and into her mouth, complicating matters. 'Gipsy! In a hole! Got to STOP THEM!'

Rounding the Maternity Ward, she had an inspiration, and turned into the Home Paddock. Just mown, with only short, fine stubble, it was much faster and safer going for Arum than the hard gravel road. Also, as the road had a distinct curve, she had a much better chance of catching the car, going straight across country. The land-rover, a hundred yards behind, had already stopped, and her father was calling out to her in astonishment. But she couldn't answer; the vet's car had almost reached the boundary fence. Through the open gate she galloped and raced on down the Clover Paddock, waving and yelling. Arum's breathing was very laboured now, but Lesley knew she had to stop that vet for poor Gipsy's sake and to make up for standing helplessly by in the bush while Val did all the work.

The Clover Paddock sped by, and the boundary fence loomed ahead of them, a tall, solid post-and-rail affair with no gate except on the road. Twenty yards away, and Lesley gave a last, desperate, breathless yell, her hopes nose-diving sickeningly as the car did not stop. Then, suddenly the idea came to her that this was also Arum's opportunity to make up, to compensate in a small way for the fact that she had made it possible for the heifer to escape. The thought of poor, exhausted, bleeding Gipsy finally decided Lesley. She galloped Arum straight at the fence. She was a jumper, wasn't she? Her only good point! Lesley took an iron grip on each rein to prevent running out, and determinedly urged on the flagging pony. The fence rushed nearer, and fear for their safety suddenly seized her. Arum – that terrible unyielding fence – broken leg – broken back? Herself – barebacked – bouncing on that bony shoulder. How horrible to hit the ground at this speed, or, worse still, to crash on to the solid posts and rails!

But Arum of the infamous one-track mind didn't falter, and Lesley couldn't have stopped her if she'd tried. She leaped like a steeplechaser; dizzily Lesley glimpsed the fence flying underneath them. They landed with a jarring thud that nearly wrenched her off-balance, and she was dimly aware of a bunch of Turners' heifers scattering in alarm as Arum careered towards the road.

'Hey! What's up, kid?'

With a tremendous effort, Lesley steadied herself as Arum bounced to a halt. She registered bewilderment at the presence of a stranger with Mr Barnett, but before she could say anything the land-rover rattled up behind the vet's car, and she was surrounded by five people demanding to know what on earth she was up to. The sixth, the stranger, said not a word, but quietly took Arum from her as she tumbled to the ground.

'It's Gipsy,' she explained for the third time that morning. 'She's stuck in a hole up at the shale works.'

'Good grief!' her father said weakly.

'Suffering cats!' said David. 'But why the steeplechase bit?'

'She's hurt. All bleeding where she's been scraping against the concrete. But now she's slipped down farther and she's not struggling any more. Val sent me to catch Mr Barnett before he went . . .' she looked around in confusion.

'And so you did,' said Mr Barnett approvingly; he was a man whom hardly anything surprised and absolutely nothing could stop talking.

But it was quite beyond Mr Mitchell to be polite now, and he ignored him. 'She's still alive, then?'

'Oh, yes! Her hips were wedged between some bits of concrete, and when we tried to move them she struggled a lot and got loose. And fell farther down the hole. Her sides are bleeding quite a bit. We were afraid she might have broken something, and then Val remembered the vet. She and Ian stayed there to prop her up and try to stop her slipping any more, so I think we'd better hurry, Dad.' She patted Arum's hot neck, told her many times that she was marvellous, and absently buckled up the throat-lash.

'We'll hurry, all right,' said her father, opening the land-rover door. 'You say there's one of those big concrete lumps half in the hole?'

'Yes, too heavy for us. Val thinks you'll need the tractor and hoist to get it out of the way and the trailer to get her home.'

'Val must be a smart girl too,' remarked Mr Barnett to

all and sundry, but he was disregarded again; what could you reply to that anyway, Lesley wondered briefly.

'How deep is the hole?' David was asking.

'Not very deep, but a funny shape and very shaley, and there's lots of concrete around. Not a bit like those eight-foot horrors, of course. Perhaps about six feet or so,' she hazarded.

'And how does Val think we'll get her out?' queried Mr Barnett with interest. This time they all heard him, and Lesley tried to remember.

'I don't think she said. But when we get the top clear of concrete – well, she's not very big, and there are three of us, and David, and Dad —'

'And Bruce,' said Bruce.

'And me, I suppose,' sighed Mr Barnett. 'But if someone drops a few tons of concrete on me, who'll mend the heifer?'

'I will,' the stranger said quietly. 'It'll be all up to me in a month, anyway.'

Lesley looked round for explanation and Mr Barnett happily obliged, introducing his replacement and cheerfully predicting that in twelve months there would be no livestock left alive in the district. During this superfluous conversation. Mr Mitchell had been working things out with David and Bruce, but now he turned to the vets.

'We'll go on ahead and get the tractor ready, if you chaps will follow? And Les, get that horse home as soon as you can without breaking her wind. You'll have to come up and show us the place.'

'I think I know it —' began David, but he was bundled into the land-rover and driven away. Still making much of Arum, but watching out for her feet, Lesley led the pony slowly along the road in the wake of the vehicles.

As it happened, she reached home very soon after they did, as Mr Mitchell had met his wife coming out to see what on earth was going on. The vets hovered helpfully round while the hayrake on the back of the tractor was exchanged for a hoist and crane, but they didn't miss the care Lesley took over walking Arum round, rubbing her down with an old towel, and administering pats and crusts and compliments before shutting her in the Pony Paddock.

'Fine pair of daughters you've got yourself,' boomed Mr Barnett in Mr Mitchell's direction. 'I'll bet it's all their brothers can do to maintain the standard!'

David caught this remark and indignantly pitched in as fast and as competently as he could, just to show the old blighter; though he too had been mightily surprised and quite impressed by Lesley's performance on Arum, and was bursting to hear how she had happened to find Gipsy. Mr Barnett cheerfully carried on about his own daughter, who was apparently also a superb rider, and Brian Robinson helped hitch the crane to the hoist.

'Boy, are we glad to see you!' said Ian's muffled voice as six people rushed into the clearing and peered anxiously into the hole. The seventh, Mr Mitchell, was bulldozing his way up from the boundary fence on the tractor.

'How is she?'

'Still O.K.?'

'Are you children all right down there?'

'So this is the wandering gipsy and the remarkable girl who tells her father what to do!'

'You've been *ages*, Les!' complained the remarkable girl from the depths of the earth. 'This cow weighs a ton! Did you stop for a sleep on the way?'

'It's only about twenty minutes since I left,' Lesley

defended herself. 'And when I got home everyone had gone but Mum. Had to go after them.'

'And then we had to get the rake off the tractor,' David explained, still being as competent as possible for the benefit of Mr Barnett.

Everyone examined the heifer and the hole and told everyone else what should be done until the tractor roared on to the platform and drowned their voices. The noise roused Gipsy a little and she lifted her head, gazing fearfully upwards and paddling ineffectually with her legs. Mr Mitchell put the tractor out of gear and came over to examine the obstacle he had to shift.

'Good thing I brought the crane up. And a good thing those bolts are cemented in this side. If they're strong enough to stand the strain it won't be much trouble to haul it away. If they're not, we'd better have a couple of levers ready in case something snaps and it falls back into the hole again.'

It was a very tense business watching the big block of concrete being hauled slowly away and expecting every second to see the rusty bolts wrenched from their sockets, letting the block fall back to its original position, or worse still, even farther. Tense for David and Bruce and Brian Robinson, waiting with strong, short saplings in case this happened. Tense for Mr Mitchell, driving the tractor, controlling the vital but dangerous power. Tense for Val and Ian and their mother, who had joined them in supporting and calming the heifer. And tensest of all for Lesley, because she had nothing to do, having been told to keep out of the way. The only person not affected in the least was, of course, Mr Barnett, who cheerfully directed operations, gave a running commentary on progress, and bent to scrutinize Gipsy when the hole was finally cleared.

'Hard to tell from up here, but I think she's all right, Jim. Looks messier than she is with all those scratches. Exhausted, though. I think you'll need those bags to make a sling to get her out.'

With grain sacks under her middle, ropes on either side, and people pulling and heaving from every possible angle, Valleywood Gipsy ascended to platform level with the minimum of effort on her part, but a great deal on everyone else's. Having set her down, they stood around breathing deeply, all smudged with black shale, and smelling of it too, while Mr Barnett did a proper examination, moving Gipsy's legs, feeling her back, and dabbing at the cruel scrapes on her hips and shoulders as she slumped prostrate on the hard ground.

'Can't find anything wrong. I'll give her an injection to boost her up, and another for tetanus.'

'But she can't get up!' cried Lesley, anguished that it had all been for nothing after all.

'No, but I'm hoping that's just due to exhaustion and exposure. Can you get a trailer up here, Jim?'

'I'll have to, by the look of things. Come on, David, I'll need a hand to get the hoist off.' Bruce offered to help too, and the tractor roared away. The others remained to do what they could for Gipsy under the vet's instructions.

'How far is the nearest water? Those abrasions should be sponged with diluted antiseptic, and I'll bet she's dying for a drink.'

'The river,' said Lesley, anxious to do something active again. 'I'll go, but what can I put it in?'

'Plenty of tins and bottles and things down at the shack,' said Val, who was propping up Gipsy's head and soothingly scratching her neck.

'Take Ian too,' Mrs Mitchell said. She was busy rubbing circulation back into the heifer's slender legs. 'And for goodness' sake rinse out whatever you find to carry the water in.'

Lesley ran all the way with Ian labouring behind, and they returned with two beer bottles each and a kerosene tin slopping between them. It was most encouraging to watch Gipsy weakly gulp about a gallon of water, easily worth aching lungs, stiff shoulders and leaden legs, thought Lesley.

'I'll give you some powder to add to her water,' Mr Barnett said, hunting for the antiseptic bottle in his case. 'It's very effective against dehydration, and she's probably suffering from that. How long has she been lost?'

'Since the night school broke up,' Val supplied. Thursday midnight, or thereabouts. About three days.'

'But if she was over the river yesterday, she can't have been here long,' reasoned Ian.

'Yes, she must have come here some time last night,' agreed Lesley, 'because I found her tracks down at the shack, and I'm sure Dad would have seen them yesterday afternoon if they'd been there then.'

'So that's how you found her,' said Mrs Mitchell, gently sponging Gipsy's hips. I've been wondering all along how you came to be up here at all.'

'We still haven't had time to look for firebug clues,' Ian pointed out hopefully, but he was squashed immediately by three quelling glances. All this naturally led to questions from Mr Barnett, and he gleaned most of the details about the fire and the search parties before the tractor and trailer arrived.

'Straw on the trailer and bags over the straw,' said Mr Mitchell, 'to save bringing the poor little devil's hips into contact with the hard wood.'

Although Gipsy was just a yearling and there were five

able-bodied lifters and four helpers present, it was quite a job to raise her from ground level to trailer level, partly because it was difficult for them to handle her without causing pain, but mainly because she was lying heavily flat-out on the ground instead of being on her feet, or at least sitting up.

'Good thing it's just a Jersey,' grunted Mr Barnett, red-faced with exertion. 'If this was a Friesian, or a beef heifer the same age, she'd still be down that hole.'

David and the young vet squeezed in at either side of the trailer to steady the heifer on the bumpy ride down to the boundary fence, and everyone else walked behind, with Mrs Mitchell and Bruce and Ian making a quick detour to see the burnt-out shack.

Although it was not yet twelve o'clock, Lesley was hot and dirty and exhausted from a morning of frantic dashing about combined with a kind of hangover from long days of searching and anxiety. And they were not over yet, she reminded herself drearily. Gipsy was found, certainly, but there was a nagging doubt about her recovery, and there was still Arum, the cause of it all, to worry about, with only about twenty dollars in hand towards the Pony Project. And all earned by Val. She herself hadn't done a thing, Lesley told herself severely, not a thing but enter that paltry competition. She rubbed her black hands absently on her tan shorts, and thought ruefully what a much better job she could have made of that story now, by introducing Gipsy's adventure into it.

'That could be a new fashion,' Val remarked, coming up from behind. 'Make a nice change from pink hearts and butterflies!'

Lesley jolted back to reality with a start. It took her a second to wake up fully, but when she did, she twisted round to both sides, saw the fairly clear shale imprints on the seat of her shorts, and grinned in spite of herself.

'Isn't it great to have found that perishing heifer at last?' Val remarked cheerfully, swinging down the steep track. 'It seems like weeks we've been looking for her, but now she is found, and the Voluble Vet reckons she'll be O.K., and Dad says that Sharon is bound to pick up after some injection or other, we can really get on with Christmas and the holidays. You can't say your old seesaw's going down now!'

'There's still Arum, she's the most important down of all.'

'Yeah,' conceded Val, 'but I don't think Dad will sell her now. I think what he said that morning was partly to scare us into keeping the old girl in, and partly a touch of harvest-time temper! Arum wouldn't bring much on account of her looks. I doubt if we have a thing to worry about, if we keep her fence mended.'

'But it's not just that.' Lesley failed to catch Val's cheerfulness. 'Even if we keep her, you know what it'll be like. Always both of us wanting her at the same time, and arguing about it.'

'Oh. I'm . . . uh . . . sorry about what I said before we came out this morning, if that's what you mean.'

Lesley sighed, watching Bruce effortlessly close the gate she had struggled with earlier. 'I'm sorry, for galloping off like that.'

'Jolly good thing you did! Otherwise we wouldn't have found Gipsy until after the vet left.'

They headed for the parked car and land-rover, the rest of the way home being navigable to ordinary vehicles. Lesley looked for a space to perch on a land-rover tray crammed with harvesting and heifer-hunting equipment. Then Mr Barnett came and invited her to ride back in his car.

'Come on!' said Ian, hauling at her shirt. It's a new Rover 2000!'

She followed rather reluctantly, silently watching the trailer rumbling ahead as Mr Barnett condescendingly rattled on to Ian about the marvels of his car. The conversation about miles to the gallon and top speeds drifted vaguely over Lesley's head until she suddenly realized the vet was talking to her.

'That was a pretty good speed you clocked on your pony this morning, young Lesley! Do you always race around like that?'

'Of course not!' said Lesley. 'That was an emergency. I didn't realize you saw,' she added, as he seemed to be waiting for her to say more.

'Oh, I picked you up in the rear vision mirror before you got to that fence, but I thought you were just clowning around. Odd-looking animal, but a pretty fair jumper, that pony of yours!'

Lesley smiled politely, aware of Ian's bewilderment, and said honestly, 'I never realised she had it in her.'

'But, as you said, it was an emergency. You jump her much?' he asked casually.

'Well . . . not very much. You see, she's just one pony between the four of us. David's left school now; he doesn't want her much, but there's Ian —'

'I like cars best,' interrupted Ian.

'— and especially Val and me. Val's older, and she sort of had her first.'

'So they both squabble all the time about who's going to ride her,' put in Ian tactlessly.

Lesley reddened and glared at him. 'It's not only that. You see, all this – Gipsy getting out and everything was really Arum's fault.'

'*Arum?* Why Arum, for Heaven's sake?'

'After Gerald Durrell's donkeys. He always says they've got ears like arum lilies, and she has, too. Anyway, she knocks fences over and opens gates, and Dad said he might have to sell her, even when she was only letting herself out. Then on Thursday night . . .'

The Rover was crawling along at the same pace as the tractor and trailer, and for once Mr Barnett seemed anxious to listen instead of talk, so Lesley, in the way of those with desperate worries, told him all about the Pony Project. As usually happens, even telling the most unlikely person helped considerably, and she felt more cheerful than she had for days, especially when the vet thoughtfully suggested weeding town gardens for the Pony Project fund.

'And I might stop by for a look at young Val's bark paintings. I haven't bought my wife anything for Christmas yet.'

'She'll be furious,' grinned Ian. 'Val, I mean. What's the best speed you've ever made in this, Mr Barnett?'

14 'Something we have to discuss'

'The thing is,' said Val practically, 'what about the reward?'

The vets had just left Guara, after cups of tea and Christmas cake provided by Mrs Mitchell and many thanks for their help from everyone.

'Any time,' Mr Barnett had said largely, with the generosity of one who is leaving the country next month. 'Makes a change from the usual run, and I must say a little gentle exercise beats sitting round reading the week-end papers.'

Gipsy was in a corner of the sick pen fenced off with hay bales. With a six-inch bed of straw, another bale behind her head, ointment smeared on her hips and shoulders, and hay and water within reach, she was as comfortable as possible. Lesley and Ian, concerned by her lack of appetite, had stayed to tempt her with grain and pellets and freshly pulled clover and anything else they could think of.

More experienced and patient with the ways of sick cattle, the other Mitchells, with Bruce, who had somehow forgotten to go home, were still inside the house, talking. At the moment the subject was Lesley.

'If only she'd told *me* when she galloped in like that,' Mrs Mitchell was saying, 'I could have got out the station-wagon and stopped everyone. If I'd just caught up with you, Jim, you could have stopped the vet; he wasn't going very fast. I nearly had heart failure, seeing her take off over the fence on that scatty mare.'

'What fence?' demanded Val, suddenly alert after spending quite five minutes grumbling about Mr Barnett's large bark-painting order.

'The boundary fence. Didn't she tell you? The vets had gone, and Dad and the boys were halfway down the road when she got here. She hardly said a word to me, just chased off over the hay paddocks after that car, yelling her head off. When they got to the boundary fence it was still going, and so was Arum. Straight over, I nearly had heart failure.'

'She jumped *that?*' yelped Val. 'Barebacked? My Sainted Aunt! Arum's wasted on hay bales – she should be in hunter trials!'

All aspects of the rescue were discussed, and Gipsy's condition, and Sharon's, and the new vet, before Val got round to asking her cryptic question.

'Surely you don't have to fork out rewards to your own family,' Mr Mitchell said hopefully.

'Which one of you did find her, anyway?' asked David.

'Oh, Lesley did. If she hadn't . . . caught Arum and gone on ahead, we wouldn't have found Gipsy in time to stop the vet. Would he have charged double if you'd had to send for him again?'

'Extra mileage. Probably. Val, does Lesley expect to land this reward?'

'I don't think she's thought of it. I didn't till just now.'

'That's good,' said Mrs Mitchell, relieved. 'Les isn't used to handling much money. It would probably go to her head to have ten dollars dropped into her lap, especially at Christmas time. I'd hate to see her waste it.'

Val hesitated, then plunged. 'I'm sure she wouldn't waste it, Mum, unless you'd call a pony a waste.'

'A pony? You mean *another* one? For ten dollars?'

'Of course. I mean, of course another one, not of course

ten dollars. Les sprung this idea on to us when we were mending the fence after Arum got out into the Home Paddock. A whole lot of propaganda about another pony helping to keep Arum from straying – company, you know. But what Lesley really wants is a pony of her own. She's crazy about riding, and, well . . . I guess I do sort of hog Arum a bit. We reckoned it wouldn't cost anything to keep another pony, once we'd bought it.'

'The Very Urgent Cause!' remembered Bruce suddenly.

'Huh?'

'I asked Lesley to tell you not to worry about my bark paintings when the heifer got lost. But she said there was an urgent reason for needing the money. I thought she meant Christmas.'

'That's why you're doing all the bark paintings, then,' said Mrs Mitchell in the voice of one to whom a mystery has been explained. 'But I haven't noticed Les up to anything.'

'She's been worrying about that. She didn't seem to be able to make a presentable bark painting, and the only other thing she's done is enter that writing thing in the newspaper. Oh, and she was talking about weeding gardens this morning. But don't tell her I've told you anything.'

'Why tell us, then?'

'Well, you were dithering about the reward, and I thought it would help Les to feel she's earned something, because she's getting pretty desperate.' (*And* because she herself had been beastly to Lesley about Arum this morning, she added privately.) 'If you can't afford it, though, Dad, she probably won't give it a thought.'

'*I* didn't know anything about this pony business,' complained David, sounding injured. 'I might have been able to help.'

'It was just after Arum got into the hay, see, and Lesley thought you'd hardly be on her side, being so wrapped up in farming and everything.'

'Why the blazes does everyone in this household assume that we're always on the verge of being broke?' Mr Mitchell suddenly inquired irritably. 'Every time money comes up, there's a sort of hushed silence from the kids, and then they sneak off and try to make it on their own.'

'Excellent for their characters,' their mother said mildly, smiling to herself.

'But damn' demoralising for my ego! What do they think I am, a ne'er-do-well, or an orgre?'

His wife laughed aloud, to Val's relief. 'It's your constant complaining about expenses, Jim, along with your endless nattering about economy and budgets. To hear you complain about calling out a vet, or having to hire extra labour, or carrying on about the harvest, *anyone* would think we were on the brink of bankruptcy!'

'Well, I'll be blowed! I'm the one that has to worry about building up the farm that keeps us all. *And* I'm trying to build up a Jersey stud too, as an extra interest for David, *and*, because I think owning more horses like that half-witted mare would be sheer lunacy —'

'Only one more, Dad,' interrupted Val soothingly, 'and of course not like Arum. She's the only one of her kind in captivity, anyway. If you'd let us have this other one, it would keep Lesley and me from each other's throats; and most likely keep Arum in her paddock, too.' She thought it was a good idea to use Lesley's own propaganda.

'Most likely eat the paddock down so much that they both get out,' grumbled her father, but he was calming down, having just recalled that there was an outsider present, and an employee at that. 'And how do you know it'll stop at one more? What about Ian? How soon will it be before he starts demanding ponies and we begin to look like a broken-down riding-school?'

'Ian's not interested in riding,' said David. 'Come the day we're silly enough to let him on the tractor, he'll never go near a horse again.'

Mr Mitchell thought about it for a moment, then grinned.

'You're a wily lot,' he said to his family. 'You wait till the weather's good, the heifer's found, the cow's getting better, and it's nearly Christmas, and then ask nicely for a pony! I suppose you'd like it delivered, gift-wrapped, on the twenty-fifth?'

Val grinned too. 'Nobody planned it that way,' she protested. 'It just happened. And I don't think there's time really, to find a pony by Christmas, Dad, with your harvest and everything.'

'How kind,' murmured her father.

'Anyway,' she elaborated, 'you don't just go out and buy a pony like a pair of socks. First you've got to find one nice and close, the right size and shape and age and colour, then you make sure Lesley can ride it and check that it doesn't buck or rear or kick —'

'Or bite,' added Bruce, deeply interested.

'That's right. Most horses have vices, not like Arum.'

'Some people would call fence-wrecking a vice,' remarked David; but Val was just getting under way, and ignored him.

'Naturally we don't need a show jumper, or a dressage horse, or even a pony club all-rounder. Just an ordinary, sensible pony, with a good eye, and nice gaits —'

'And a nice price?' suggested her father.

'That's what I was worried about,' said Mrs Mitchell. 'Not just the price, but if Lesley gets a pony for

Christmas, Ian will expect a new racing bike, Val will want a colour movie outfit, and goodness only knows what David will ask for.'

Val and David both protested at once, but Mr Mitchell grabbed at a straw and drowned their outburst by saying loudly, 'A very good reason for leaving this matter till after Christmas. As you say, Nancy, earning a bit of money for something they want badly will be a jolly good thing for the kids. We'll see how they go, and perhaps make up the difference later on, when they find a pony they think is a possibility.'

The phone rang, and Mrs Mitchell got up. Glancing to the clock, however, she headed for the sink instead of the hall, saying, 'Will you get that, Jim? I should have the dinner on.'

Val reluctantly got up to help her wash vegetables. David reluctantly got up and said he'd go and see how the kids were getting on with Gipsy. Bruce got up most reluctantly of all and said he really must be going, but Mrs Mitchell invited him to stay to dinner, so he and David promptly sat down again and began talking about tomorrow's harvest. It was quite ten minutes before Mr Mitchell reappeared.

'Lesley in yet?' he asked. 'No? Good. There's something we have to discuss. That was the vet . . .'

Heather Barnett was seventeen and fair and pretty, and not one hundred per cent wrapped up in the idea of leaving Tasmania. It was partly the home she was used to, partly all her friends, and partly her pony. Although Matric. studies and exams had meant that she hadn't found much time to ride him in the past year, the prospect of selling him, now that it was looming quite alarmingly, was suddenly too awful to think about. The pony had been advertised for sale and a couple of people had tried him out, but Heather had refused to let him go either to the timid little boy who hung on to his mouth all the time, or to the older girl, who had a reputation for her daring show jumping and would no doubt over-face him. Dad kept pestering her about the gruesome subject, and now he was at it again, expounding the virtues of some country kid he had just met.

'Now look here, hon, you know we've got to sell him. Can't take him to Europe, and let's face it, you've hardly ridden him for months. He's getting old and fat and lazy. That's a hell of a waste of a good horse.'

'I know, Daddy. Don't keep on at me! I couldn't let him go to that horrible Gibbs girl, now could I? And the little boy yesterday couldn't ride for nuts. They'd have ruined each other.'

'Fair enough,' conceded her father. 'And that's what I'm trying to tell you. This kid I've found doesn't go in for showing or pony clubs or anything fancy. She's got it all without that – all except the pony. Her sister's, the one she was riding, is the weirdest looking clown of a horse you could ever hope to see, but it's in good condition. The Kid – Lesley, she's called – found a sick heifer up in the bush, and came down to get me to have a look at her. But Brian and I had just left, so she came galloping across country to stop us. Went clean over a post-and-rail fence barebacked, on this horse that doesn't look as if it could jump a brick.'

'Sounds like a speed maniac,' said Heather dismissively.

'Just what I thought. But when I was talking to her afterwards – just casually – she sounded quite horrified at galloping so far. An emergency, she said; she wouldn't have dreamed of doing it normally. I led her on a bit, and found she was trying to save money to buy a pony.

Apparently they're not terribly well off, but she didn't have any wild ideas. She said a rough pony to school would be O.K.'

'You couldn't call Shadow that!'

'Of course not!' agreed Mr Barnett hastily, aware that he had put his foot in it. 'But think what a windfall he'd be to this kid, at such a bargain price. She'd treasure him, really look after him. On a farm, too, instead of in a pokey little town paddock. All their animals are well looked after. I think Lesley's the right kind of rider for him. Enough guts to keep him going properly, but good light hands and common sense as well.'

'Um. You didn't offer him to her, did you?'

'Of course not. But we've got to get a move on, Heather. We're leaving in a month, and we can't spend the last few days frantically trying to place your horse. They'll be hectic enough without that. Now, let me give her father, Jim Mitchell, a ring and see what he says. He may not be interested; then we'll have to look for someone else. But if he is, I reckon Shadow's found his new home. Lesley's a jolly nice kid – and they're a jolly nice family.'

A sceptical frown clouded his daughter's pretty face, but the disconcerting fact that parents are so often right had been proved to her before, usually to her lasting embarrassment or regret. The cloud passed, and she smiled reluctantly.

'O.K., Daddy. Trot out the Country Wonder and I'll cast a critical eye over her.'

'There's a good girl.' He stooped and kissed the top of her head on the way to the phone.

In less than ten minutes he was back.

'What time would suit you best to let the Mitchells come along and try him out?'

15 The bush lease

If Lesley had happened to overhear either of these conversations, her feelings would have been virtually indescribable, but of course she didn't, so her feelings remained as describable as before: mingled relief and worry, thankfulness that school was over, and impatient anticipation of Christmas and the summer holidays, when the hectic harvest would be finished and only ordinary chores would interrupt swimming and riding and reading in the sun.

On Monday morning, to everyone's relief, Gipsy began to eat. Not very much, but at least she was drinking large quantities of water containing the vet's powder to stave off dehydration. Lying in the deep straw bed of the sick pen, she accepted mainly bran (combined with one or two nourishing ingredients that Mr Mitchell had come up with), and handfuls of fresh clover pulled from the cow pastures. Mixed with their relief was an undercurrent of anxiety that she still couldn't get up, though she managed to change her position all through the morning, moving round the pen like a baby learning to creep. Even this was more of a nuisance than otherwise; not only did it keep opening the sores on her hips, but it meant frequent visits to the sick pen were necessary to move her feed buckets around so that they were always within her reach.

This job fell mainly to Lesley and Ian, as Val was furiously manufacturing bark paintings, and Mrs Mitchell was continuously manufacturing meals to keep the harvesters going. They required gallons of chilled drinks, too, for the sun was blazing and the humidity so intense that Smiler was having the time of his life forecasting doom and destruction in the form of thunderstorms, and so irritating Mr Mitchell that he was seriously considering employing someone else for the job next year. When Val came into the Ten Acre bearing a tray of drinks and humming a Christmas carol she'd just heard on the radio, she caught one of Smiler's more drastic prognostications (a cloudburst before tomorrow), and was inspired to bestow on him the title of 'Comfort and Joy'. It seemed more suited to the time of year than 'Smiler', and so much better than calling him ... what *was* his real name, anyway?

Passing round the drinks, she managed to pass around the new name as well, somehow imparting it to everyone but the unsuspecting Mr Hodgets, who sat in the shade with an expression like that of a morose bloodhound, but who nevertheless managed to put away two large glasses of iced cordial. Everyone agreed that the new title was most apt.

When Lesley came indoors from the sick pen, she was surprised to hear from her mother that a friend had phoned to invite her to go Christmas shopping in Devonport.

'You weren't here, dear, but I said you'd like to; I know you haven't done any yet.'

Although she seldom resorted to it, Mrs Mitchell was a most convincing liar, and Lesley never learned the truth – that her mother had actually telephoned Betty Anderson to arrange to have Lesley out of the way for the afternoon. Despite this, Lesley was a little puzzled.

'What about Gipsy, though, if I go to Devonport?' she asked.

'Ian's still around, isn't he? Or Val can run out and check on her every so often.'

'Oh, aren't they going too?'

'No. Ian wasn't asked, and Val wants to keep on with her bark painting. Run and put on something clean, dear. They're coming to pick you up soon.'

Lesley ran along, more puzzled than ever. Jenny Anderson was nearly fourteen, more Val's friend than her own. Climbing into her lightest pair of clean jeans and a sleeveless top, however, she remembered yesterday morning Val's voiced intention of giving everyone bark paintings. That was why she was staying home, of course. Scraping together hoarded remnants of pocket-money into her purse, Lesley wondered vaguely whether Ian and David would really appreciate bark paintings for Christmas. Brushing her hair into a pony tail, she concluded that must have been one of Val's sweeping statements; she would no doubt have something more suitable in mind, for her brothers at least.

Lesley sighed and got out her own Christmas list with its five names in a column and suggestions opposite. Ian was easy. He was always losing his pocket-knife or handkerchiefs or fish-hooks – it was just a matter of replacing one or other of these items. Dad was easy, too, because he always kept a farm diary and she bought him a new one every Christmas. Mum would be pleased with anything. The only difficulty there would be choosing from all the attractive ideas displayed in the shopping-centre. David was much more difficult.

'Val, what do you want for Christmas?'

Val grinned, looking up from her bark. 'The very latest Glen Campbell album and a nice portable record player to play it on!'

'I mean from me.'

'Oh. Um. I don't know. How about a new paintbrush? This one reckons it wasn't meant for gluing bark. It's going bald, losing hair all over the place. Next thing it'll be staging a sit-down strike!'

Lesley made a note of that, and was going to ask Val's opinion about David's present when Mrs Anderson's car drove into the yard.

'Have a good time, Les!' Val waved the unsatisfactory paintbrush after her fleeing figure. But the car had scarcely turned out of the farm road before she flung it down and raced to find her riding boots. About twenty degrees too hot for them today, she thought, but it's vital to make a good impression.

Lesley did have a good time, mainly thanks to the three dollars her mother had given her before she left, and the fact that the very first thing she found was a book for David, by his favourite author. Milking was in progress when she got home, so she concealed her bag of parcels and went out to help feed the calves. Val had a very smug expression about something, but Lesley, feeling rather smug herself after her successful afternoon's shopping, didn't notice, or if she did, she put it down to Val's cheerful news.

'Sharon's improved out of sight, even since this morning. She's actually eating and milking again. And there are two new calves, both heifers. Linda and Milkmaid. And we've got in all the Ten Acre —'

'How's Gipsy?'

Val's cheerfulness abated some two degrees. 'About the same. The Voluble Vet said not to try to get her up until she shows signs of wanting to.' The two degrees returned with fifty per cent interest. 'But what I keep trying to say is that Dad's sold the hay in the Shale Paddock – to Mr McGuire, because most of his was burnt.'

'That's nice,' said Lesley, missing the point. 'Oh! How much do you sell hay for?'

Val was pretty hazy about this, but she said convincingly enough that it depended on whether the hay was standing or baled '— and I s'pose it'll be baled, as it's already cut.'

'How much, then?'

Val admitted defeat, and ran over to the dairy to ask David, leaving Lesley having her bare knee licked by Guara Supreme while Tassel hovered nearby, hopefully waiting for the order to drive him away.

'Fifty cents a bale,' reported Val, coming back, 'and Dave says a good average cut is seventy-five bales to the acre.'

'The Shale Paddock's the biggest one, isn't it? Fifteen acres. That's seventy-five times fifteen. Oh, heck, can you multiply by fifteen – in your head, I mean?'

'Val couldn't, so she did it in the dust, much to Tassel's interest. 'One thousand, one hundred and twenty-five bales times fifty cents. That's . . . um . . . five hundred and sixty-two dollars, fifty cents, if it's a good average crop.'

'Cripes!' Hay to Lesley had always been a common substance that you filled the calves' racks with, or used to wipe the muck off your shoes, or for bedding in Ian's guinea-pig cages. During the harvest worry she had come to realise that large quantity was vital to the cows in winter, but she had never thought of it in terms of hard cash before. 'Over five hundred and sixty dollars!'

Val checked her arithmetic again, because Tassel had walked on the bottom line. 'That's right. But don't carry on about it. Dad's pleased, but he's not excited. I mean, it sounds like a fortune to us, but all farming things are madly expensive. Think of the wages for Bruce, and old

Comfort and Joy, and goodness only knows what it costs to keep the harvesting machinery going.'

On Tuesday morning the deluge of summer calves got really under way with a tiny bull born during the night and another heifer soon after breakfast. Mr Mitchell left his calves with their mothers for only one night, so calf-feeding was becoming quite an involved job, with bottles and teats and colostrum for the babies, and skim-milk and buckets for the older ones. In between carting in the hay from the last paddocks (for the second storm prophesied by Smiler never happened), regular checks had to be made among the cows for milk fever and calving problems.

When Val wasn't helping or bark-painting or Christmas shopping, she spent a great deal of time schooling Arum Lily, getting her quite fit through exercise in the heat. Furious at being forbidden to try Lesley's jump, the boundary fence, she had bullied Ian into helping her build yet another wobbly series of hurdles and walls in the Pony Paddock, and was training Arum over these, despite David's dire predictions that it would only teach her to jump fences on her own. To Val's credit, Arum was performing quite impeccably, except for the time she sampled the brush jump instead of jumping it, and the temporary fall from grace when she leaned against a tottery hurdle while Val was dismounted to raise a pole.

Amidst all this activity, the job of feeding Gipsy during the day often fell to Lesley, and she was the one who first found the injured heifer on her feet.

It was Tuesday afternoon and, watching Val on Arum, Lesley had suddenly thought about the writing competition she had entered. She had never expected to win anything, of course. Nevertheless, she went into her bedroom and fished out the hoarded newspaper with the entry conditions in it. 'Closing date . . . results published 17th December.' Three days ago! Now, what did Mum do with the old newspapers in summer when there were no fires to be started? Incinerated them, probably, after a decent interval. But surely, Saturday's paper . . .

She leafed through the magazine rack, looked on the kitchen bench, fumbled behind and underneath the living-room chairs. *The Advocate*, Tuesday 20th. Today's. Monday 19th. Yesterday's. The 16th, the 14th, *The Advocate* . . . But she couldn't find Saturday's paper anywhere. Where else? Val's desk, of course! Newspaper spread under all those bits of bark. She ran back to investigate, but that was dated the 10th, positively ancient.

'Silly idiot,' Lesley told herself. 'You'd have been notified, anyway, if you'd won anything. Don't start telling yourself how much work you put into that dumb story. You never expected to do any good with it. Arum's O.K. at the moment. In the new year you'll really do something to earn money. Something sensible. No, stop *thinking* about the competition. Remember that Gipsy's found now, and Sharon's getting better.' Gipsy! It was about time she took her a drink – and Lesley went out of the back door.

With the automatic efficiency of one doing a routine job, she filled a bucket with water, pulled a handful of leaves from the willow-tree as a special treat for Gipsy, and swung round the corner of the sick pen where the heifer was lying in the shade. But she wasn't lying in the shade. Transfixed with astonishment and disbelief, Lesley almost dropped her bucket at the sight of Valleywood Gipsy standing stiffly in the doorway, watching her approach.

'Gipsy!'

Half-afraid to move, Lesley crept forward slowly, remembering how a sudden movement had caused the heifer to slip farther into the hole at the shale works. But now Gipsy was mellowed by two days of almost constant human service and companionship. Besides, she was so stiff that her joints creaked with every movement. And on top of all this, the timidly advancing human was offering willow leaves, the most succulent of all treats. Gipsy took two creaky but eager steps towards Lesley and curled her tongue around the fresh leaves. Flooded with relief, Lesley took three steps out into the sunshine. So did Gipsy, anxious for attention and willow leaves. The bunch of leaves was flung on the ground at her feet, but all she got in the way of attention was a quick rub behind the ears before Lesley turned and ran, at top speed despite the heat, to find someone, everyone, and tell them about it.

When she found the whole family in the last hay paddock, she was slightly daunted by the presence of a strange car at the end of the track, and two outsiders talking to Mr Mitchell. But as she approached, the two strangers got into the car and drove away, and Mr Mitchell strode to meet the land-rover, which was heading across the paddock carrying a full load.

'Hoy! HOY!'

Everyone stopped and looked at Lesley, then past her as if they expected to see the house on fire. Seeing nothing of the sort, they transferred their collective gaze back to Lesley again, and called out almost in unison, 'What's up?'

Lesley ran to meet them. 'Gipsy's up! On her feet! Come and see!'

'She's not!'

'Really!'

'Thank goodness for that!'

'I *am* glad, dear.'

'Can she walk?'

'This I must *see*!'

'Come on, then. The load's full, anyway.'

Mr Mitchell deliberated a moment, then nodded, and the eight of them headed out of the Dry Paddock – in the cab, on the load, or on foot.

Gipsy had made her way out into the yard, looking for the herd mates she had missed so long, but a complication had occurred. The Mitchells arrived just in time to see her confronted by Tassel, who knew perfectly well that she didn't belong there but was uncertain of what to do about it, being a well-trained dog who acted on orders only. Gipsy, wide-eyed but unafraid, had lowered her head to sniff at Tassel, and Tassel's expression was an interesting one of combined indecision and wariness of the probing muzzle. At the approach of the family, she waved her tasselled tail and looked up hopefully for human arbitration in this delicate situation. But it was a long time coming. The humans, for some inexplicable reason, complicated matters still further by standing round laughing. In some ways, this was a relief; at least it transferred the attention of that terrible sniffing muzzle, and the puzzled dog was able to make a more or less dignified retreat to the safety of behind David's legs. But it was quite ten minutes before things returned to normal and the offending animal was removed to a proper and fitting place for a cow.

'I think she'll be all right there,' Mr Mitchell said, closing the Maternity Ward gate after Gipsy. 'I'll shut her in the sick pen for the night, out of the way of the maternity cases, and if she's all right in the morning we'll turn her out into one of the calf paddocks.'

He turned to go and help Bruce and Smiler, who were unloading in the barn, but Mrs Mitchell stopped him. 'Jim, what brought the Police Sergeant out to see you this morning? And who was that man with him?'

'Oh, was that the Sergeant?' said Lesley, who hadn't seen him before.

'Well, among other things, he cleared up the fire Mystery!' Mr Mitchell grinned at Ian, who was wide eyed with interest.

'Apparently it's connected with a pair of no-hopers McGuire found having a grog party in his barn a couple of weeks back. Naturally he pitched them out, and their bottles after them, but one of them retaliated that Friday night, when the McGuires were out. Anyway, someone talked, and by some miracle the Sergeant got on to them.'

Mrs Mitchell sighed. 'Vandals. Fancy setting fire to a man's barn with no reason other than that. Kids just didn't do that sort of things when I was young.'

David interrupted hastily, having heard this one many times before. 'You don't mean he came all the way out here just to tell you that, Dad? Who was the other man?'

Mr Mitchell sighed. 'Bloke called Trevor Jackson,' he said, enlightening neither his wife nor his children. 'From the Mines Department.'

They waited expectantly. He grinned reluctantly. 'You prying lot. No respect for a man's private affairs.'

'We never said a thing,' said Ian indignantly, 'though Val's practically dying to.'

'Well, we can't have that. Might need her later.' Jim Mitchell's grin broadened as he eyed the near-bursting Val. 'I was going to discuss it tonight, anyway. Jackson's offered me the lease of the bush. The mines are outdated, of course, and now the Caretaker's gone, so —'

'The lease! Just what does that entail?'

'Listen and I'll tell you. It would mean, to all intents and purposes, that the whole lot would be ours – to plough and sow down, and perhaps clear the higher parts later. It's a godsend, really. What with the river and the town as boundaries, and Turners owning the rest, the only way the farm can hope to expand is to the south. We ought to grab this opportunity with both hands.'

'What's the catch?' Mrs Mitchell asked sceptically. 'It's not like you to be enthusiastic about money outlay.'

'Well, apparently leasing defunct Mines land as opposed to the Department employing caretakers is their way of cutting down on expenses. We get full use and full responsibility for it, and the yearly rent is very reasonable. You've got to look at it as an investment. Think of the extra young stock that block could carry, even if we only sowed the flats. With that part for the dairy cattle, we could turn those ti-tree paddocks along the creek into pasture for the herd and —'

'Milk more cows,' David broke in excitedly. 'We could build up twice as quickly, and sell twice as much milk.'

'We could ride all over it with that Caretaker gone!'

'But what about all those terrible holes?' protested Mrs Mitchell. 'I could never let you ride near them, and we certainly don't want any accidents there.'

'We'll fill them in,' said Val.

'Fence them off,' said David.

'Both, I think,' said Mr Mitchell. 'Fill in any rough places on the flats and fence off the Shale Hill part till we can bulldoze it.' He smiled complacently at his wife.

'Well . . . have you accepted this offer?'

'Of course not, without consulting anyone. Though I knew you'd all be pleased, of course. I'm to ring up tonight to accept it. And now we'd better go and help those blokes unload. Come on, David!'

'And now I know where Val gets it from,' said Mrs Mitchell dazedly, watching her husband and son stride away before starting back to the house.

'Gets what?' said Ian, looking wonderingly at Val, who pulled a face at him.

'That sneaky way of pretending they're discussing things with you when they've really made up their minds ages ago,' explained Lesley perceptively. 'They squash everything you say, then tell you what to do, and get out of the way quickly so there's nothing you can do but do it.'

Ian frowned in his effort to sort this out, but Mrs Mitchell looked searchingly at Lesley with a quite startled fancy-you-knowing-that expression. 'That's exactly what they both do, Les!'

Val grinned. 'Listen to the pot calling the kettle black. You're just the same, Mum, when you're on to us about doing homework. And David does it, too, when he wants us to help with his farm jobs.'

'I don't think I ever do it,' said Lesley, frowning.

'Then it must be a tendency that creeps in as old age approaches,' teased her mother.

'Can't be,' said Val, ' 'cause Ian's the worst of the lot of us at wriggling out of things and getting his own way. And *that's* why Les doesn't do it – because Ian's the only one around for her to order about, and he's far too good at passing the buck to obey any orders. He's so sharp he's practically out of sight before you can open your mouth.'

Fortunately for family peace, Ian, having run on ahead with Tassel, was out of sight when Val voiced this theory. But as they rounded the barn he came running back, announcing in a hoarse, conspiratorial whisper, 'There's a car at the back gate. A *blue mini*!'

'Auntie Joy!'

'Joyce.' Mrs Mitchell sighed. 'Oh, dear, just look at us all. Les, you look as if you haven't changed your shorts since they got all over shale on Sunday.'

'I don't think I have,' said Lesley cheerfully, twisting round to look. 'But Ian looks like one of Finnelberry Huck's poor relations!'

'Fin —? Oh, I see. Well, what about yourself, Mum?' Val said, before they got around to her. 'That tatty old shirt with paint all over it, and *must* you wear those mucky shoes around the place?'

'Well, it's too hot for gumboots, and I wasn't going to wear decent shoes to take drinks out to the hay paddocks,' her mother said defensively. 'But I must say it's a pity. Quite apart from making *me* feel dowdy and dirty, your aunt always lays down the law about the way I let you lot get around, and how I should bring you up properly and set a good example. She just doesn't understand about farms.'

'She didn't see me,' said Ian hopefully. 'Let's all do a right-about turn and go and help the men unload.'

'Ian! I *must* be bringing you up badly! This is your *aunt*, paying her Christmas calls, most likely. You're all to come in and be *polite*, but just see if you can do something with a comb and hot water first, please.'

'I must say I can't see the point of Christmas calls,' whispered Lesley to Val and Ian as they sneaked in the back way. 'Sitting around being polite when everyone's so busy.'

'Christmas calls – oh, My Sainted Aunt!' exclaimed Val appropriately. 'She must have come for her bark paintings!'

'Well, you've got them ready, haven't you?'

'Yes, ready to post down to her!' said Val, fetching

them from her desk. Unfortunately, her loud exclamation had attracted their aunt, who appeared in the bedroom doorway just as Val snatched the brown paper wrapping off her parcel.

'Hallo, Lesley, Valerie! I thought for a moment there was nobody here.'

'I think Mum's in the kitchen,' said Val, hearing the distant clatter of afternoon-tea noises as she dutifully submitted to being kissed.

'Dears, I'm in a *tearing* hurry. I haven't even time for a cup of tea. I just called in to collect my bark pictures. Is that what you have there, dear? I told you I'd collect them.'

She reached out her hand for the parcel; divested of the outer brown paper, the bark paintings were padded round with newspaper.

'Val, that paper,' Lesley said. 'What date —'

At this precise moment, everyone was interrupted by Ian's voice blasting urgently through the house.

'Val! *Les*! Arum's in the vegetable garden! Oh, hurry *up*!'

'Excuse me, Auntie!' Val leapt into action, like a spurred horse. Horrible visions of trampled vegetables and parental wrath coursed through Lesley's mind, so devastatingly clear that she scarcely registered the disappearance of the parcel into Auntie Joy's handbag before diving after Val.

16 The seesaw at its highest

'Merry Christmas!' said David a trifle sardonically at an unearthly hour on Sunday morning.

Whatever happened to prevent them on ordinary Sundays, the Mitchells always made a determined effort to go to church on Christmas morning. Unfortunately, this required a very determined effort indeed, as the minister, a country parson, had to hold Christmas morning services at four churches, and the very first of these was at eight o'clock, at the Mitchells' church, which was by far the nearest to Guara. Thus, while other families lay in bed, or were noisily dragged out by present-seeking children, the Mitchells were hard at work ticking off the various jobs that had to be done before church. Chief of these was, of course, milking, accomplished in record time by Mr Mitchell and David, with special extra help from Mrs Mitchell, who later left them finishing up to help Val and Lesley with the baby calves, which by Christmas morning numbered twelve. Miscellaneous jobs such as chook feeding and driving the cows to their paddock fell to Ian, who was last up owing to having been last to go to sleep the previous night.

Breakfast before church was really quite unworthy of the name; it consisted of bananas and chunks of bread and cheese bolted hastily while everyone climbed into tidy summer clothes and washed off any bits of dirt that showed.

A frantic scramble for collection (which they never did remember to get out the night before), an undignified rush for the station-wagon, and they made it, filing into a back pew just as the first hymn was announced. Mr Mitchell, unusually well-groomed and handsome in his only suit; Mrs Mitchell looking young and pretty in a yellow dress she had made herself; David spruce in pressed trousers and a cheerful coloured shirt his father didn't approve of; Val with pigtails tied up in red ribbon to match her floral print dress (which clashed abominably with David's shirt); Lesley in a new blue frock with her hair brushed out; and Ian as neat and combed and well-behaved as a small boy in a television commercial. This lasted throughout the entire familiar service, the last roof-lifting chorus of 'Come, All Ye Faithful', and the usual exchange of greetings and pleasantries outside the church before they piled into the car again and Mr Mitchell loosened his tie, Val kicked off her shoes, which pinched, and Ian shed his innocent air by observing as they drove away, 'Isn't it lucky Christmas is on a Sunday this year? It sort of kills two birds with one stone! Dad, the street's practically deserted and you're only doing thirty. Couldn't you sort of step on it a bit?'

'The suspense is killing him,' grinned Val; but Lesley noticed that she was almost bouncing on her own seat. With holiday amiability, Mr Mitchell increased their speed to forty until the turn on to the Guara road forced it down to twenty again, much to Ian's disgust.

Ian had been agitating for ages to change the Christmas routine, and was irritated by the fact that no one had seriously considered his suggestions of getting up at half past four in order to have presents before Church, or, alternatively, to go to a later (much later) church service somewhere else instead of to the local one. Now, positively unable to wait another second, he was galloping into the house even before the car engine was turned off, leaving handkerchief and hymn-book in his wake. Mrs Mitchell smiled indulgently as she bent to pick them up; she emerged with a handful of envelopes as well.

'Friday's mail,' she explained rather sheepishly, adding it to her armful of gloves and handbag and hymn-books. 'It must have got pushed down the side of the seat by a box of groceries, or something. Come on, Val! Ian will demolish the whole Christmas-tree if we don't hurry!'

'Talking of demolishing, I think I want breakfast almost more than presents!' Val said; but she didn't seem in much hurry for either, Lesley noticed; she kept gazing back the way they had come as if she were looking for something.

Lesley always thought of Christmas day in four stages: the first – hard work and haste; the second – church, with a calming effect, but an undercurrent of excitement; the third – the Christmas-tree, where the mysteries of the past few weeks were revealed; and fourth – Christmas dinner, after which what they did was usually dictated by the fruits of stage three.

Ten minutes later, the third stage was under way, and the fruits becoming apparent. At least, Ian's fruits were. As they came into the living-room after a quick change into their cleanest jeans and shirts, Val and Lesley and David narrowly missed being blinded by the flying end of a new fishing-rod wielded by their young brother.

'Hey, look out! If you don't go easy with that thing I won't be able to see my presents!'

'Oh, sorry, Dave. But isn't it a beauty!' And Ian charged past to thank his parents, who were making a second breakfast in the kitchen.

Lesley always loved to watch other people opening their presents, especially when they were the ones she had chosen herself, so she unwrapped her own parcels slowly, while her mother thanked her for the new purse and soft blue scarf she had finally picked, and exclaimed satisfactorily over Val's bark painting. Mr Mitchell was astonished to receive a bark painting too, and highly amused at its subject – three or four crudely-shaped bark cows running in all directions with their tails flying, and a harrassed, two-legged stick figure tearing his hair behind them. 'The day I breed a cow that looks like that, I'll give up!' he laughed, then thanked Lesley for her diary, and David and Ian for a wallet and half a dozen rather startling handkerchiefs.

Fortifying herself with a mug of milk coffee and chunks of rich Christmas Cake, Val was attacking her presents with a speed that would have done Ian credit. There was something funny about Val this morning, Lesley thought, as her sister grinned widely with joy and ran to put her coveted record on the player, with plenty of volume. It wasn't like Val to hurry through her presents like that. She glanced across at David, but he was behaving normally enough, sitting at the table with her book and a new shirt that caused the one he was wearing to pale into insignificance, making appreciative thanking noises through a mouthful of Christmas cake. Ian was wallowing hopelessly amongst a sea of papers for something he might have missed.

Lesley's first parcel was a rather hopeless bottle of bathsalts from Auntie Joy, and her second pair of kneesocks, but the third was really worthwhile – a big, well-illustrated book about horses, with chapters on riding, showing, breeding, stable care, ailments; it covered everything, she thought, browsing happily through a section on schooling that would no doubt be very useful when . . .

At this point, with the record player temporarily silent while Glen Campbell paused for breath, she heard a screeching whinney. For one swift moment she thought it was something she had imagined through force of suggestion, but everyone else had stopped what they were doing, and Val had run to take the needle off the record.

Oh, Arum! *Please* don't get out today! Lesley hurried to the window that looked out on the Pony Paddock, but halfway there was stopped by a neigh from the other direction, and whirled round in confusion. Help! Where had that dratted mare got herself now?

Then there was a loud knock at the back door.

'I'll go,' Lesley called out; she was halfway there, anyway. She flew out through the hall, wondering where was the most sinful place Arum could possibly have got to, because there she would undoubtedly be found, and snatched the door open.

The man on the doorstep was the Voluble Vet, and he started being voluble right away. 'Merry Christmas, young Lesley. I dare say I could have dug up a red suit from somewhere, but no power on earth would get me into white whiskers, so I'm just the delivery boy.'

Unfortunately this speech was entirely lost on Lesley, who, unaware of her family crowding round behind her, was staring, utterly flabbergasted, at a point three feet to the right of Mr Barnett. Standing there, ears pricked at Arum's shattering whinneys, was a big, almost white pony, with dapples on his quarters and a brown rope halter on his head. Lesley knew he was real because she had blinked hard twice, and both times he had still been there when she opened her eyes.

'What's the matter, don't you like him? Isn't he big enough? White enough? Pretty enough? Let me tell you, young lady —'

The rest of Mr Barnett's volubility was drowned by the pony, who lifted his clean-cut white head and gave another shuddering, ear-splitting neigh in reply to Arum, who was still yelling her head off in the Pony Paddock. This clinched the fact that he was real, and Lesley turned dazedly to her parents, who both smiled back at her, confirming the wonderful, unbelievable truth. But still she went on not very brightly saying nothing, though she was blinking furiously and trying desperately to find some words.

'Don't you think he's beautiful, darling?' her mother helped her out, understanding.

'You'd jolly well better!' said Mr Mitchell; but he was still grinning.

'I've been absolutely almost exploding with the secret for a whole *week*,' said Val exultantly, 'but you never guessed, did you?'

'I think Val wanted to hide him under her bed,' grinned David, 'but Mr Barnett offered to deliver him right on the day.'

Ian was getting impatient. 'Go on, Les. He's all yours. Do something. *Say* something!'

Lesley stared back at the pony, and suddenly there were a hundred things she wanted to say. But first she turned on her parents and hugged them both so heartily that they were reduced to breathlessness.

Mr Barnett sighed in an exaggerated way. 'This is all very well, but how long do I have to stand here being a hitching-post for this animal?'

Lesley grinned at him joyfully and took the halter rope and rubbed the white nose. 'What's his name? How old is he? He's just gorgeous, Mum! But how on earth, I mean, why? I just don't get it!'

Nor did she for some time, because everyone began to

talk at once, telling her about the reward, how Mr Barnett had seen her boundary-fence jump, been impressed by the Guara animals, and had rung up to offer Shadow at a bargain price if they could persuade his daughter to part with him.

'Which wasn't too easy,' said Val. 'She knew she couldn't take him to England, but she was pretty choosey about his new home.'

'She didn't like the idea of not meeting the actual prospective new owner,' explained David, 'but Mum and Dad wanted Shadow to be a surprise, so Mr Barnett praised your riding to the skies, and I'm afraid Val dopped you in to write and send progress reports to Heather when she goes to England.'

'We went out to try him the day you went to Devonport,' said Mrs Mitchell, 'and Mr Barnett offered to bring him today, straight after church. I was terrified he'd be late and we'd have to explain why you had hardly any other presents!'

'We thought you'd rather we all collaborated on this one, along with your Pony Project—'

'So we did,' said Val, 'but I'm never going to make another bark painting, ever.'

'I never even noticed about the other presents,' said Lesley, 'but I won't need Christmas presents for about ten years after this. What's he like to ride, Val?'

'Oh, splendificent! You'll have to try him straight away. I rushed like a mad thing to open all my presents before he came, so now we can go and introduce him to Arum. She'll be a pretty hoarse horse if we don't shut her up soon!'

Suddenly terribly impatient, Lesley made to lead Shadow away, but caught her mother's meaning glance in time, and stopped.

'Oh, um, Mr Barnett. Thank you ever so much for bringing him down and everything. And please thank Heather and tell her I'll look after him. And I'll write, too!'

Mr Barnett grinned at her and slapped Shadow's back dismissively. 'As I've said before, Jim, you've a fine pair of daughters.' He raised his voice. 'There's a little saddle out in the horse-box, Lesley. No use to us now . . .' then lowered it again. 'Yes, thanks very much, Mrs Mitchell. A cup of coffee would go down very well.'

The introduction went off smoothly, Arum being the mildest of ponies, really, and Shadow the perfect gentleman. Then they went for a ride. A preliminary trot down the lane, then both were pounding across the Ten Acre, heading for the bush. And nobody minded that they weren't back in time to help get the Christmas dinner.

'I feel as if I'll positively burst if anything else happens,' said Lesley several hours later, leaning back in her chair after describing at great length what a marvellous ride Shadow was, and how well he got on with Arum.

'I reckon you'll positively burst anyway if you don't stop eating,' her father said, in an attempt to change the subject of conversation that had remained the same throughout the whole meal of cold ham and salad with strawberries-and-cream meringue and coffee and nuts and glace fruit to follow.

But Lesley still persisted. 'Isn't it funny,' she said, 'that proverb about an ill wind? If Sharon had never got sick, the vet would never have come here before he went away to England.'

'It wasn't Sharon, it was Gipsy,' contradicted Ian. 'If she hadn't been hurt up in that hole, the vet would never have seen Arum in action.'

'And if *you* hadn't found Gipsy, Lesley, we wouldn't have considered giving you the reward,' Val pointed out.

'The vet would still have rung up,' said Lesley.

'But Dad mightn't have accepted his offer,' said Mrs Mitchell. 'Not if Val hadn't brought up the subject of ponies and rewards just before.'

'No, it all comes back to Gipsy,' Val insisted hastily. 'If she hadn't got lost, none of it would ever have happened.'

'But *Arum* let her out,' said David, 'so really you've got her to thank.'

'For goodness sake, stop all this analysing!' Mr Mitchell intervened irritably. 'It's like a vicious circle, always coming back to that blasted mare.'

Before her daughters could fly to the defence of the blasted mare, Mrs Mitchell sighed and said loudly, 'Well, girls, I'm afraid the table won't clear itself.'

As she scraped back her chair, a pile of envelopes fell to the floor. 'Oh, those letters! I've been sitting on them!'

Reprieved, Val and Lesley reached for more raisins while she sorted Friday's mail. 'All Christmas cards, I think, and one for Lesley. Who do you know in Hobart, Les?'

'Only the cousins there,' said Lesley, reaching out eagerly. Letters for her were very few and far between, even at Christmas time.

'Oh, dear,' murmured Mrs Mitchell over her last Christmas card. 'The Carters, Jim, I don't think I sent them one.'

'Bit late now,' her husband rejoined lazily. 'They probably . . . what's up, Les? Who's it from?'

'I don't know . . . I think it says . . . But I don't quite . . .'

'A cheque!' Her father seized the slip of paper that had fluttered into her lap. 'For twenty dollars! What on earth!'

'Oh, is that a cheque? I . . . Val, it's that competition in the *Advocate*! I've won a prize for my poem! There's an awfully nice letter from that author type I hadn't heard of. He says congratulations on my simple but au-then-tic (whatever that means) poem, and it's going to be printed! "Enclosed is a cheque for . . ." ' She laughed ruefully, though her eyes were shining with triumph. 'Isn't it queer? I worried for weeks about not earning any money, then I got my pony out of the blue, and then *this*!'

'The seesaw at its highest!' teased Val, getting up to read the letter over her shoulder. 'Though really it's just a coincidence that this came right on top of everything. One of our forgetful Mama's slip-ups!'

Mrs Mitchell smiled ruefully. 'All this seems too much excitement for one day – especially Christmas day!'

By the time the letter had gone around the table, Lesley was positively starry-eyed with modest pride. 'If I hadn't gone out to watch Supreme being born—' she began.

'For Pete's sake, don't start that again,' interrupted her father. 'If *you* hadn't been born it wouldn't have happened either! "Is that a cheque?" ' he murmured disbelievingly. 'To think that my ignorant daughter's never even seen one!'

'What I'd like to see is a copy of this poem,' said David with brotherly scepticism.

'Yes, darling,' said Mrs Mitchell. 'I'd love that too – oh, blow, the phone!'

She departed to the hall and returned five minutes later.

'Auntie Joy wants to talk to you, Les. Don't forget to thank her for the bath-salts!'

Lesley went dutifully, but was soon back. 'She said, Merry Christmas, congratulations on the poetry prize and why didn't we tell her before. And she wants Val now.'

'But how did she know about the prize?' asked Ian, fearing that it would be his turn next.

'The paper with the results – last Saturday's paper, the one I couldn't find – Val had wrapped her bark paintings in it. And Auntie J saw my name in the paper late last night when she was unwrapping them.'

'Oh. I hope Val remembers to thank her for the talcum powder.'

Lesley opened the door to remind Val, but was just in time to hear her do it.

'—lovely, Auntie, I really liked it. What's that? *How* many? But I – no, really – Yes, Auntie. I can't! Oh, very well. Sure, Auntie. Right-o, I'll get him. Bye-bye!'

She came back to the kitchen and flopped down with a Smiler Hodgets expression on her face. 'Ian, you're wanted.'

Ian went resignedly.

'Comfort and Joy,' said Lesley. 'What's up, Val?'

Val sat up dramatically. 'Don't talk to me about joy. Auntie Joy was "delighted" with the bark paintings and so were the unutterable people she gave them to. And she wants five more, FIVE MORE, *big ones*, for some American tourists who are leaving in the New Year! Ow! I feel like murdering someone – probably you, Les. If you hadn't got us started on this darn Pony Project, I'd never have *heard* of bark paintings, and if Auntie Joy hadn't—'

'For Heaven's sake!' roared her father. 'Stop this blasted iffing!'

'What's iffing?' demanded Ian, coming back. 'You now, David.'

'Iffing,' began Val, then exchanged gleeful glances with Lesley and they both began laughing, oblivious of their mystified brother. But Mrs Mitchell wasn't.

'Ian! Did you thank Auntie Joy for the socks?'

'Oh, did she give me the socks? I thought that was someone else. I thanked her for the book on fishing. She did sound a bit surprised.'

'*Ian*! If only you'd keep tabs on the labels when you unwrap them!'

'Next year,' said Ian vaguely. 'What did she give you, Les?'

'A bottle of bath-salts.'

'Oh. Talking of bottles, it was my idea to go up to the Caretaker's shack after clues. If I hadn't thought of that, we probably never would have found Gipsy, and Mr Barnett would never—'

He broke off, wondering what he had said to make Dad glare at him and his two mad sisters laugh so loudly that there was no point in going on. Whatever it was, he decided it was best not to say any more. He reflectively debated the merits of almonds or figs or raisins, and finally reached a highly satisfactory compromise by cramming his mouth with a delicious mixture of all three.

These are other Knight Books

Mavis Thorpe Clark

PONY FROM TARELLA

In the summer Sandy had been on holiday from the orphanage at Tarella Station where he befriended the beautiful and spirited golden-brown mare, Sunflower. Everyone said she was a one-man horse and he hoped one day to buy her. But when he returns to Tarella for his next holiday he is hurt to discover that Sunflower has been promised to Phil. Sandy is no longer allowed to ride her and has to watch as she is bullied into obedience by Phil . . .

Primrose Cumming

SILVER SNAFFLES

'Through the Dark Corner, and the password is Silver Snaffles,' said the old pony Tattles to Jenny. He takes her to a secret riding stables where the ponies can talk and where they teach her to ride, as she has always longed to do. She soon makes friends with them and has many adventures which she will never forget.

These are other Knight Books

Ruby Ferguson

'Jill' books remain the most popular and delightful pony books of all.

JILL'S GYMKHANA
A STABLE FOR JILL
JILL HAS TWO PONIES
JILL ENJOYS HER PONIES
JILL'S RIDING CLUB
PONY JOBS FOR JILL
JILL AND THE PERFECT PONY
ROSETTES FOR JILL
JILL'S PONY TREK
